# EVALUATION FOR RISK
# OF VIOLENCE IN ADULTS

## BEST PRACTICES IN FORENSIC MENTAL HEALTH ASSESSMENT

### Series Editors

Thomas Grisso, Alan M. Goldstein, and Kirk Heilbrun

### Series Advisory Board

Paul Appelbaum, Richard Bonnie, and John Monahan

### Titles in the Series

Foundations of Forensic Mental Health Assessment, *Kirk Heilbrun, Thomas Grisso, and Alan M. Goldstein*

#### Criminal Titles

Evaluation of Competence to Stand Trial, *Patricia A. Zapf and Ronald Roesch*

Evaluation of Criminal Responsibility, *Ira K. Packer*

Evaluation of Capacity to Confess, *Alan M. Goldstein and Naomi Goldstein*

Evaluation of Sexually Violent Predators, *Philip H. Witt and Mary Alice Conroy*

Evaluation for Risk of Violence in Adults, *Kirk Heilbrun*

Jury Selection, *Margaret Bull Kovera and Brian L. Cutler*

Evaluation for Capital Sentencing, *Mark D. Cunningham*

Eyewitness Identification, *Brian L. Cutler and Margaret Bull Kovera*

#### Civil Titles

Evaluation of Capacity to Consent to Treatment, *Scott Y. H. Kim*

Evaluation for Guardianship, *Eric Y. Drogin and Curtis L. Barrett*

Evaluation for Personal Injury Claims, *Andrew W. Kane and Joel Dvoskin*

Evaluation for Civil Commitment, *Debra Pinals and Douglas Mossman*

Evaluation for Harassment and Discrimination Claims, *William Foote and Jane Goodman-Delahunty*

Evaluation of Workplace Disability, *Lisa D. Piechowski*

#### Juvenile and Family Titles

Evaluation for Child Custody, *Geri S.W. Fuhrmann*

Evaluation of Juveniles' Competence to Stand Trial, *Ivan Kruh and Thomas Grisso*

Evaluation for Risk of Violence in Juveniles, *Robert Hoge and D.A. Andrews*

Evaluation for Child Protection, *Karen S. Budd, Jennifer Clark, Mary Connell, and Kathryn Kuehnle*

Evaluation for Disposition and Transfer of Juvenile Offenders, *Randall T. Salekin*

# EVALUATION FOR RISK
# OF VIOLENCE IN ADULTS

KIRK HEILBRUN

OXFORD
UNIVERSITY PRESS

2009

# OXFORD
UNIVERSITY PRESS

Oxford University Press, Inc., publishes works that further
Oxford University's objective of excellence
in research, scholarship, and education.

Oxford New York
Auckland   Cape Town   Dar es Salaam   Hong Kong   Karachi
Kuala Lumpur   Madrid   Melbourne   Mexico City   Nairobi
New Delhi   Shanghai   Taipei Toronto

With offices in
Argentina   Austria   Brazil   Chile   Czech Republic   France Greece
Guatemala   Hungary   Italy   Japan   Poland   Portugal   Singapore
South Korea   Switzerland   Thailand   Turkey   Ukraine Vietnam

Published by Oxford University Press, Inc.
198 Madison Avenue, New York, New York 10016
www.oup.com

Oxford is a registered trademark of Oxford University Press

Library of Congress Cataloging-in-Publication Data

Heilbrun, Kirk.
Evaluation for risk of violence in adults / Kirk Heilbrun.
p. cm. — (Best practices in forensic mental health assessment)
Includes bibliographical references and index.
ISBN 978-0-19-536981-6
1. Violence—Risk assessment. 2. Dangerously mentally ill—Risk assessment.
3. Forensic psychology. I. Title.
RC569.5.V55H45 2009
614'.15—dc22

                                                                2009000051

9 8 7 6 5 4 3 2 1

Printed in the United States of America
on acid-free paper

*To the memory of Saleem Shah.*
*I hope you would be pleased with how risk assessment has developed,*
*and know you would not be satisfied.*
*Both the advances and the demand for improvement are part of*
*your legacy to the field.*

# About Best Practices in Forensic Mental Health Assessment

The recent growth of the fields of forensic psychology and forensic psychiatry has created a need for this book series describing best practices in forensic mental health assessment (FMHA). Currently, forensic evaluations are conducted by mental health professionals for a variety of criminal, civil, and juvenile legal questions. The research foundation supporting these assessments has become broader and deeper in recent decades. Consensus has become clearer on the recognition of essential requirements for ethical and professional conduct. In the larger context of the current emphasis on "empirically supported" assessment and intervention in psychiatry and psychology, the specialization of FMHA has advanced sufficiently to justify a series devoted to best practices. Although this series focuses mainly on evaluations conducted by psychologists and psychiatrists, the fundamentals and principles offered also apply to evaluations conducted by clinical social workers, psychiatric nurses, and other mental health professionals.

This series describes "best practice" as empirically supported (when the relevant research is available), legally relevant, and consistent with applicable ethical and professional standards. Authors of the books in this series identify the approaches that seem best, while incorporating what is practical and acknowledging that best practice represents a goal to which the forensic clinician should aspire, rather than a standard that can always be met. The American Academy of Forensic Psychology assisted the editors in enlisting the consultation of board-certified forensic psychologists specialized in each topic area. Board-certified forensic psychiatrists were also consultants on many of the volumes. Their comments on the manuscripts helped to ensure that the methods described in these volumes represent a generally accepted view of best practice.

The series' authors were selected for their specific expertise in a particular area. At the broadest level, however, certain general principles apply to all types of forensic evaluations. Rather than repeat those fundamental principles in every volume, the series offers them in the first volume, *Foundations of Forensic Mental Health Assessment*. Reading the first book, followed by a specific topical book, will provide the reader both the general principles that the specific topic shares with all forensic evaluations and those that are particular to the specific assessment question.

The specific topics of the 19 books were selected by the series editors as the most important and oft-considered areas of forensic assessment conducted by mental health professionals and behavioral scientists. Each of the 19 topical books is organized according to a common template. The authors address the applicable legal context, forensic mental health concepts, and empirical foundations and limits in the "Foundation" part of the book. They then describe preparation for the evaluation, data collection, data interpretation, and report writing and testimony in the "Application" part of the book. This creates a fairly uniform approach to considering these areas across different topics. All authors in this series have attempted to be as concise as possible in addressing best practice in their area. In addition, topical volumes feature elements to make them user friendly in actual practice. These elements include boxes that highlight especially important information, relevant case law, best-practice guidelines, and cautions against common pitfalls. A glossary of key terms is also provided in each volume.

We hope the series will be useful for different groups of individuals. Practicing forensic clinicians will find succinct, current information relevant to their practice. Those who are in training to specialize in forensic mental health assessment (whether in formal training or in the process of respecialization) should find helpful the combination of broadly applicable considerations presented in the first volume together with the more specific aspects of other volumes in the series. Those who teach and supervise trainees can offer these volumes as a guide for practices to which the trainee can aspire. Researchers and scholars interested in FMHA best practice may find researchable ideas, particularly on topics that have received insufficient research attention to date. Judges and attorneys with questions about FMHA best practice will find these books relevant and concise. Clinical and forensic administrators who run agencies, court clinics, and hospitals in which litigants are assessed may also use some of the books in this series to establish expectancies for evaluations performed by professionals in their agencies.

We also anticipate that the 19 specific books in this series will serve as reference works that help courts and attorneys evaluate the quality of forensic mental health professionals' evaluations. A word of caution is in order, however. These volumes focus on best practice, not what is minimally acceptable legally or ethically. Courts involved in malpractice litigation, or ethics committees or licensure boards considering complaints, should not expect that materials describing best practice easily or necessarily translate into the minimally acceptable professional conduct that is typically at issue in such proceedings.

This book attempts to synthesize the important developments in violence risk assessment with adults, particularly over the last two decades. It does not describe risk assessment with juveniles or with sexual offenders; both are addressed by other books in this series. It does, however, place violence risk assessment within the particular context of FMHA—so those using this book will find it useful in considering best practices in FMHA risk assessment, but not necessarily for risk assessment that is performed in other contexts.

Alan M. Goldstein
Thomas Grisso
Kirk Heilbrun

# Acknowledgments

I gave my first workshop in risk assessment for the American Academy of Forensic Psychology in 1991. An intensive review of the literature had yielded a handout that was 18 pages long (including references). My current iteration of this handout approaches 150 pages; even that cannot provide in-depth consideration of many of the facets of risk assessment that have developed in the last two decades. This is one illustration of how risk assessment has grown, matured, and advanced empirically over this period. A book on best practice reflects these advances, to which many have contributed. First are the researchers, scholars, and practitioners who have contributed to these advances. Many of you are referenced in this book, as you have authored studies or written conceptual or applied articles. Others do not appear in the "literature," but your contributions have been likewise important: considering these advances, applying them in your practice, teaching, and training, and struggling to reconcile the advances with the continuing limitations. I thank all of you.

The American Academy of Forensic Psychology (AAFP) has been a model for exemplary continuing education and advocacy for forensic practice at the highest levels. AAFP has been an important collaborator in this best practice series—appropriate, considering their modeling of forensic best practice—and I am grateful to the Academy for all they have done with this series and, more generally, for forensic mental health assessment. Alan Goldstein and Randy Otto deserve particular thanks for the work they do in directing the AAFP continuing education series. Alan and Tom Grisso also served as action editors for this book, and were unfailingly succinct, incisive, and timely throughout this process. It has been a great pleasure to work with both of them on this series. I also thank John Monahan and Kevin Douglas for their comments on this book and the ideas contained in it; it is much better as a consequence.

Finally, I am grateful to my wife, Patty Griffin, and our daughter Anna, for their love and patience—and for making my life so much better than it would otherwise be.

# Contents

# FOUNDATION

# The Legal Context

**1**

Violence is a very significant problem in our society. It is directly related to public safety and the perception of safety, one of the most fundamental priorities for a legal system. Unlike most of the other issues that are addressed by books in this series for best practices in forensic mental health assessment (FMHA), however, the risk of violence is not an ultimate legal question to be answered by the judge. It is considered in various criminal, civil, and juvenile/family decisions made by the courts. In this respect, it is more like the broad notion of "legal competencies" (Grisso, 2003) than one specific kind of competency. Appraising the risk of future violent behavior, and sometimes the needs for interventions that would reduce that risk, is part of FMHAs associated with a range of legal questions. The particular details of this appraisal are what distinguish one *risk assessment* from another.

This book will address best practice in the evaluation for risk of violence in adults. (Another book in this series will do the same for juveniles; see Andrews & Hoge, in press.) Because of the wide range of legal questions that focus on violence risk, this book does not attempt to provide a detailed review of violence risk assessment in the context of each legal question. Instead, the emphasis will be on violence risk assessment as a process—including the steps that are indicated, the role of specialized risk assessment tools, the scientific and applied debates surrounding this area, and the integration of risk assessment into the evaluation.

## Sociolegal Purpose and History

The present priority on public safety manifests itself in a variety of ways. Individuals with severe mental illness who decline treatment can no longer be involuntarily hospitalized for treatment needs alone, but "danger to self or others" remains a cornerstone of U.S. civil commitment statutes. Defendants at different stages of the criminal justice system—from diversion to hospitalization, from sentencing to transfer within correctional facilities to release—may all be evaluated for their risk of harm to others as part of the particular legal decision. Thus it is not surprising that risk assessment has been one of the areas in which the law has most often sought expert opinions from mental health professionals.

However, this is a topic on which mental health professionals have not always had useful contributions. The American Psychiatric Association (1982), in an *amicus* brief filed in the U.S. Supreme Court case *Barefoot v. Estelle* (1983), argued that psychiatrists had no particular expertise in predicting *dangerousness*, as the Texas statute called on them to do in the context of capital sentencing:

> Psychiatrists should not be permitted to offer a prediction concerning the long-term future dangerousness of a defendant in a capital case, at least in those circumstances where the psychiatrist purports to be testifying as a medical expert possessing predictive expertise in this area. . . . The forecast of future violent conduct on the part of a defendant in a capital case is, at bottom, a lay determination, not an expert psychiatric determination. To the extent such predictions have any validity, they can only be made on the basis of essentially actuarial data to which psychiatrists, *qua* psychiatrists, can bring no special interpretive skills. (p. 3)

Indeed, a review of Monahan's seminal (1981) book entitled *Predicting Violent Behavior* provides a good idea just how problematic this professional task was at the time. The tone of the book was constructively critical but not nihilistic—though Monahan noted in the foreword that his working title had once been "Predicting Violent Behavior: Why You Can't Do It." It is fortunate that he decided that perhaps you could do it, but a tremendous amount needed to be accomplished in the field before it could be done reasonably well. His book marked a major shift in the scientific and professional approach to the task of appraising the risk of future violent behavior. Monahan provided conceptual clarity, described the needs for supporting empirical evidence, and outlined guidelines for the mental health professional. He subsequently refined many of these ideas, and collaborated in providing much of the necessary data, that transformed the "prediction of dangerousness" to "violence risk assessment and risk management" in the nearly three decades that have passed since he wrote this book.

One of the important issues addressed by Monahan (1981) was the use of actuarial versus clinical approaches to predicting violence. A more contemporary view involves comparing structured approaches versus unstructured professional judgment (Monahan, 2008). These are discussed in some detail in this book. There have also been other important contributions since 1981; these will be described next.

## The Algebra of Aggression

Megargee (1982) described four domains that influence whether an individual will engage in criminal violence: *instigation, inhibition, habit strength,* and *situation.* The first, instigation, is the sum of internal influences (thoughts, feelings, motivations, and the like) that incline an individual to behave violently. Inhibition, by contrast, is the sum of the internal influences that make it less likely that an individual will display violent behavior. Habit strength describes that individual's history of violent and nonviolent behavior, while situational influences refer to factors that are not internal, including location, the presence of others, and the ingestion of drugs or alcohol. Megargee's description was important for several reasons. Violent behavior is complex and multi-determined; the algebra of aggression provides a way of classifying these influences by domain, and considering how and where intervention is needed to reduce the risk of such behavior. It also prompted researchers, clinicians, and forensic evaluators to consider each domain. Situational influences on violence, for example, can be potent—but have received less empirical and professional attention than they deserve, as will be noted next.

## Situational Influences

Just as Megargee described the importance of situational influences on violent behavior, Steadman (1982) provided a more detailed perspective on the contributions of context to violence risk. Researchers paid little attention to this domain in the 1970s. While context should receive more empirical scrutiny than it does, the influence of situations on violence risk has become much better recognized. Appraisals of risk have become better focused on situational considerations such as the location of the individual being evaluated (hospital or prison vs. community). Some specialized risk assessment tools prompt the user to describe the transition between hospital and community (see, e.g., the Risk section of the HCR-20; Webster, Douglas, Eaves, & Hart, 1997). There are even measures that incorporate situational aspects of risk for those in hospitals (Ogloff & Daffern, 2006) and prisons (Cooke, Wozniak, & Johnstone, 2008), as well as empirical research on the influence of neighborhood on violence risk (Silver, 2001). The consideration of situational influence is now an accepted part of FMHA risk assessment—a marked shift from how "dangerousness" was assessed as recently as two decades ago.

## Shorter Outcome Periods

The period of time over which a legal decision maker is considering the risk of future violence varies across legal questions. In civil commitment, for example, this period is measured from hours to months, while the outcome period of interest for individuals in post-sentence *Hendricks* commitments for sexual offenders is far longer. Beginning in the 1980s, consistent with Monahan's (1984) call for a "second generation" of research in violence, we began to see studies using outcome periods of 6–12 months rather than the far longer

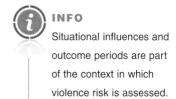

outcomes often used in previous research (see Otto, 1992, for a summary). This research allowed a better empirical foundation for FMHA evaluation of legal questions with outcome periods of varying lengths.

**1**
chapter

## From Dangerousness to Risk Assessment

"Dangerousness" was the term most often used to describe the focus of this type of forensic assessment before the 1990s. This term continues to be used in legal language, but researchers and scholars have become more precise when describing their target behaviors. "Dangerousness" has at least three components: *risk factors* (variables empirically associated with the probability that aggression will occur), *harm* (the amount and type of aggression being predicted), and *risk level* (the probability that harm will occur) (National Research Council, 1989). Using the term "risk assessment" promotes disaggregation of these components. Speaking of "dangerousness" does the opposite (See Figure 1.1). When an

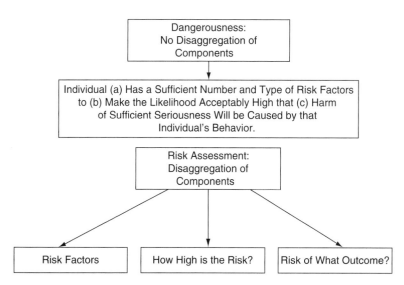

**Figure 1.1**   Dangerousness vs. Risk Assessment

evaluator concludes that an individual is dangerous, such an opinion reflects the view that the evaluated individual (a) has a sufficient number and type of risk factors to (b) make the likelihood acceptably high that (c) harm of sufficient seriousness will be caused by that individual's behavior. All three of these components have unspecified values ("a sufficient number," "acceptably high," and "sufficient seriousness") that are filled in by the evaluator providing an opinion concerning the individual's dangerousness. "Risk assessment" immediately begs three questions: Risk of what outcome? How high is the risk? What influences contribute to the risk? For reasons of increased specificity, decreased reliance on one's own values, and better risk communication, researchers and scholars (e.g., Monahan & Steadman, 1994), and subsequently forensic clinicians, have substituted "risk assessment" for "dangerousness" in FMHA.

## Risk-Needs-Responsivity

Outlining three distinct concepts—risk, needs, and responsivity (RNR)—was one of the important conceptual steps provided at the end of the 1980s (Andrews, Bonta, & Hoge, 1990). *Risk* refers to the principle that those most likely to engage in future crime should receive the most intensive intervention and management services. *Needs* are deficits related to the probability of such outcomes, called criminogenic needs in the RNR model as they relate to the risk of reoffending. *Responsivity* refers to the individual's likelihood of responding to intervention(s) designed to reduce the risk of criminal reoffending. A subsequent distinction between prediction and risk management (Heilbrun, 1997) emphasized the legal context of different decisions, with some focused on prediction and others on both risk appraisal and risk reduction. Risk assessment approaches emphasizing prediction tended to use mostly *static risk factors* (without the potential to change through planned intervention), while those focused on both risk appraisal and risk reduction needed to include *dynamic risk factors* (having the potential to change through planned intervention) as well. The RNR approach provided the conceptual foundation for the development of *risk-needs tools* such as the Level

**INFO**

The RNR model outlines three distinct concepts:

- Risk: targets those most likely to engage in future crime

- Needs: deficits related to the probability of such outcomes

- Responsivity: factors related to response to interventions

of Service Inventories (LSI-R; Andrews & Bonta, 1995; LS/CMI; Andrews, Bonta, & Wormith, 2006) and the HCR-20 (Webster, Douglas, Eaves, & Hart, 1997). The distinction between prediction and risk management allowed a clearer description of those legal contexts in which *prediction only* was appropriate, and other legal questions in which *both prediction and management* were indicated. This allowed a more informed selection of specialized risk assessment tools, depending upon whether the legal question focused on prediction or both prediction and management.

## Public Health Influence

Prior to the 1990s, research and scholarship considered violent behavior almost entirely within the context of crime and offending. A shift then occurred to analogizing violent behavior to health problems such as cancer and heart disease. Thus, it became more straightforward to conceptualize violence in terms of risk factors and protective factors, and to address the prevention of violence as well as the rehabilitation of those arrested for criminal violence. This also expanded the range of influences that investigators considered in research on violence, and moved the definition of "outcome" from acts that resulted in criminal sanctions (arrest or conviction) to behavior that could be described by self-report, collateral report, or official records.

## Increased Analytic Sophistication

The difference between a research study on dangerousness conducted in the 1970s and a risk assessment study in the twenty-first century is substantial. One of the important differences involves the influences of decision theory. This involves classifying outcomes in terms of positives (predictions that violence will occur, subclassified as either *true positives*—correct predictions—or *false positives*—mistaken predictions that violence will occur when it actually does not) and negatives (predictions that violence will not occur, subclassified as either *true negatives*—correct predictions—or *false negatives*—mistaken predictions that violence will not occur when it actually does). These classifications of predictive accuracy can be summarized using *sensitivity* (the number of true positives divided by the sum of true positives and false negatives) and *specificity* (the number of true negatives divided by the sum of true negatives and false positives). Further, Receiver Operating Characteristic (ROC) analysis is typically used in contemporary violence risk research. This analysis depicts the true positive rate as a function of the false positive rate for a given evaluator. It also measures the overall accuracy of a judgment or a technique in distinguishing violent from nonviolent individuals without being affected by base rates or evaluators' preferences for certain outcomes (e.g., false positive preferred to false negative) (Mossman, 1994).

## Expanded Classes and Range of Risk Factors

A systematic description of risk factor domains was provided by one group of investigators as part of the MacArthur Risk Assessment project, funded by the MacArthur Foundation and conducted in the late 1980s and 1990s. Four classes of risk factors were described: *individual* (demographic, personality, and neurological), *historical* (family, work, psychiatric, criminal, and aggression), *contextual* (social support and physical aspects of environment), and *clinical* (mental disorder, substance abuse, and global level of functioning) (Steadman et al., 1994). These domains were also used by investigators who were developing specialized risk-needs tools, so the risk factors (and protective factors) began to show considerable overlap across populations. Consider the HCR-20 (Webster et al., 1997) versus the LSI-R (Andrews & Bonta, 1995), developed for appraising risk of violence in populations with severe mental illness and risk of reoffending in a general offender population, respectively. Both tools include items focused on risk reduction as well as risk level. Despite the somewhat different target outcomes and populations for which these tools were developed, they overlap in a number of respects (see Table 1.1). This overlap of domains and specific items reflects a fairly substantial

**Table 1.1** | Examples of Domain Overlap for Risk Assessment Tools

| LSI-R | HCR-20 |
|---|---|
| Criminal History | Previous Violence/Prior Supervision Failure |
| Education/Employment | Employment Problems |
| Alcohol/Drug Use Problems | Substance Use Problems |
| Family/Marital | Relationship Instability |
| Arrested Under the Age of 16 | Young Age at First Violence |
| Emotional/Personal | Personality Disorder and/or Psychopathy |
| Attitudes/Orientation | Negative Attitudes |
| Companions | Relationship Instability and/or Lack of Personal Support |

consensus within the field regarding broadly applicable areas of risk factors for violent behavior and criminal offending.

# Violence Risk Assessment: Legal Contexts

## Forensic Mental Health Assessment

Violence risk assessment is not associated with a single legal question. In this 20-volume series, at least half of the books address some aspect of risk assessment. We have chosen to address the broad issues surrounding risk assessment with adults in this book, and risk assessment issues with juveniles in a separate book (Andrews & Hoge, in press).

There are other legal contexts as well. Individuals found *Incompetent to Stand Trial* (*IST*) and committed for secure hospitalization may need to satisfy a "dangerous to self or others" criterion as part of such hospitalization. There are other kinds of forensic evaluations that can assist the decision maker in determining whether an individual meets the criteria for transfer from a correctional setting (jail or prison) to a secure hospital. Likewise, the decision maker must determine that an individual no longer meets criteria as "mentally ill and dangerous to self or others" for that individual to be returned from a secure hospital to a correctional setting. Release decision making involves a similar decision that an individual's risk of violence toward others is acceptably low. However, the less structured community setting to which the individual will be transferred is substantially different from a correctional facility—so the nature of the risk assessment in such release decisions differs as well.

There is an additional domain of risk assessment which is distinct from those described in the last paragraph. When individuals who remain under the jurisdiction of a court or correctional system are treated to manage their risk of violence, the ongoing measurement of treatment progress should include some kind of risk-needs assessment. This means that there must be some focus on the "needs" of the individual that affect the risk of a certain outcome.

## Risk of Harm to Identifiable Third Parties

Outside the scope of FMHA, risk assessment also includes when the therapist is concerned about the patient's potential for serious harm to an identifiable third party. In the first of two California cases that have subsequently been expanded to other jurisdictions, the court held (in *Tarasoff*, 1974) that the therapist has a duty to "warn" third parties about potential violence by a client if the victim is identifiable and the therapist "knows or should have known" that violence would occur. The second *Tarasoff* holding (1976) expanded this duty. In this decision, the court required the treating mental health professional to use reasonable care to "protect" the potential victim of client violence when that professional determines (or should have determined, pursuant to the standards of the profession) that the client will harm an identifiable third party.

There is an interesting parallel between the prediction/risk reduction dichotomy noted earlier and the obligations attached to the mental health professional through each of these decisions. In the first, the treating mental health professional is asked to assess the risk that the client will actually harm the identified third party— and act to convey the risk to that individual through a warning. In the expanded duty to protect outlined in the second *Tarasoff* decision, the court endorsed a variety of steps that could be taken to manage this risk and thereby protect the third party. The implications for mental health professionals in avoiding *Tarasoff* liability have been described in detail elsewhere (see Monahan, 1993). Decisions made in a therapy context regarding a client's risk of harming a third party differ in some important respects from the risk assessment procedures described in this book, although some of the research and procedures may be relevant.

**CASE LAW**

*Tarasoff* (1974)

- Established that a therapist has a duty to "warn" third parties about potential violence by a client if the victim is identifiable and the therapist "knows or should have known" that violence would occur

*Tarasoff* (1976)

- Required the treating mental health professional to use reasonable care to "protect" the potential victim of client violence when that professional determines (or should have determined, pursuant to the standards of the profession) that the client will harm an identifiable third party

# Legal Standards

It is not meaningful to discuss legal standards—statutes, case law, and administrative code—for "risk assessment" broadly. Such standards differ according to legal question, and cannot usually be generalized across legal questions. It is important, therefore, to discuss legal standards for risk assessment in association with particular considerations that combine to distinguish a particular type of FMHA risk assessment. There are five such considerations that commonly arise, and it is useful to consider how they apply to such legal standards. Three of these were noted earlier in this chapter, in describing how the field has moved from using the term "dangerousness" to using "risk assessment" instead. All five considerations are (a) nature of risk factors or indicators of risk, (b) level of risk, (c) severity of the harm (physical aggression only? threats of harm? any illegal behavior?), (d) length of the outcome period, and (e) context in which harm may occur. These are considerations that have substantially influenced researchers, scholars, and practitioners to focus on "risk assessment," specifically defining these considerations. Legal standards typically remain less specific and continue to use the terms "dangerous" and "dangerousness," however.

**INFO**

The five main considerations for risk assessment in relation to legal standards are

1. Nature of risk factors or indicators of risk

2. Level of risk

3. Severity of the harm

4. Length of the outcome period

5. Context in which harm may occur

This is not to suggest that the law should define its terms differently. Fundamental differences between philosophies underlying law and science, respectively, promote flexibility and individualized decision making in our legal system and precise, reliable operationalized definitions in science. The attempt to impose a scientific or clinical epistemological framework on the law has long been identified as an error of intrusiveness (Grisso, 1986). But what is the relationship between dangerousness and violence risk? What does best practice

**BEWARE**
Legal standards of "dangerousness" may use outcomes that are somewhat different than those considered in violence risk assessment.

suggest when the law speaks of dangerousness, and forensic psychology and psychiatry focus on risk assessment?

It is important to consider the questions noted in the first paragraph in this section. The answers to these questions provide information that is relevant to a decision maker's determination of whether an individual is dangerous. But evaluators should bear in mind that the legal term "dangerous" may encompass more than violence toward others, even when threats are included. As will be discussed with respect to criminal responsibility ( *Jones v. United States*, 1983), some legal standards use criteria for "dangerous" that include any criminal offending. This underscores the importance of clarity on the behaviors included within the "target" of what is being assessed. Such a range may be gauged from a review of relevant statutes, case law, and administrative code within a particular jurisdiction.

The relationship between the questions included in risk assessment and the ultimate determination of an individual's dangerousness is part of the broader debate on *ultimate issue testimony* (concerning whether the expert should give an opinion on the "ultimate legal question" before the court). One suggested resolution, applicable when ultimate issue testimony is required, involves (a) providing all necessary supporting information (in this case, answering risk-relevant questions using information from the risk assessment), (b) noting the distinction between the advisory role of the evaluator and the decision-making authority of the court, and (c) answering the question ("is this person dangerous?") in light of (a) and (b) (Heilbrun, Grisso, & Goldstein, 2008). It is important to consider the various standards associated with different legal questions. Several important standards for specific legal questions will now be discussed.

## Correctional Transfers

The question in this area is whether due process entitles a convicted offender to notice, an adversary hearing, and representation by counsel before he/she is involuntarily transferred to a state mental hospital for the treatment of mental disease or defect. The U.S.

Supreme Court held that such notice and adversary hearing were necessary but counsel was not (*Vitek v. Jones,* 1980). The applicable standard for correctional transfers involves the presence of mental illness and serious threat of harm to self or others. This is not much more elaborate than "dangerous to self or others," although it does imply that the risk must be elevated ("serious" threat). The nature of the risk factors, severity of possible harm, and length of the period under consideration are not specified. As is typical in statutes on involuntary civil commitment, the risk to both others and to the individual himself is considered. *Vitek* provides precedent for correctional transfer statutes but not necessarily for the definitions relevant to risk assessment; the Court's decision addressed the Fourteenth Amendment Due Process considerations involved in the transfer, not the nature of the transfer criteria.

## Criminal Responsibility Hospitalization and Release

In *Jones v. United States* (1983), the U.S. Supreme Court considered a case that involves the nature of "dangerousness" as it applies to individuals committed as *Not Guilty by Reason of Insanity* (*NGRI*). The question concerned whether Mr. Jones, who had been committed to St. Elizabeth's Hospital following an insanity acquittal for stealing a jacket, was entitled to release or a less restrictive form of commitment (civil commitment) after a period of hospitalization equal to the maximum length of sentence that could have been imposed upon conviction. The

Court held that he was not so entitled—he should remain hospitalized until he has "recovered his sanity" or is no longer dangerous. This decision contained language that helped clarify how the Court was considering the concept of "dangerousness." The majority opinion held that committing a criminal act "certainly" indicates dangerousness, a category which encompasses a variety of acts. The opinion also observed that the Court has never held that violence in particular (as contrasted with the larger category of "dangerousness" outlined in this decision) was a prerequisite for involuntary commitment to be constitutional. In terms of the five questions noted at the beginning of this section, the *Jones* decision addressed the nature of the harm that is the target of the assessment. "Dangerousness" is implied by the risk of *any* criminal offending, not simply by that of violent behavior or violent offending, in the commitment criteria for those acquitted by reason of insanity.

The second relevant case involving dangerousness and the commitment of individuals acquitted by reason of insanity is *Foucha v. Louisiana* (1992). This case considered the question of an individual, also acquitted by reason of insanity, who appeared to have "regained sanity" but continued to be dangerous due to his antisocial personality disorder. On that basis, the Court held an individual could not continue to be involuntarily hospitalized solely because of continued dangerousness. Both prongs of the commitment criteria—mental illness *and* dangerousness—must be met. This decision elaborated on the source of the dangerousness, particularly the nature of the risk factors. The risk of harming others associated with antisocial personality disorder alone may be comparable to (or greater than) the risk posed by mentally ill individuals within insanity acquittees as a group. The level of this risk was not relevant to their decision, however. Rather, the Court held that when one of the two necessary commitment criteria is not present, then continued involuntary commitment is not justified.

**CASE LAW**

*Foucha v. Louisiana* (1992)

● held that both prongs of the commitment criteria—mental illness and dangerousness—must be met to justify involuntary commitment following acquittal by reason of insanity

## Capital Sentencing

The jury in a capital murder trial in Texas must respond affirmatively to "special issues" after a defendant has been convicted. One of those issues involves whether the defendant is likely to commit criminal acts of violence that would constitute an ongoing threat to society. All states using the death penalty employ a framework that involves the consideration of aggravating and mitigating circumstances, which individualizes the sentencing decision. Such individualized consideration has been required since the U.S. Supreme Court determined, in a series of three cases (*Gregg v. Georgia*, 1976; *Profitt v. Florida*, 1976; *Jurek v. Texas*, 1976), that capital sentencing is constitutional. Texas, however, is unusual in explicitly citing risk of harm to others as a factor to be weighed in the capital sentencing process. That may help to explain why three of the important cases in this area originated in Texas.

In *Estelle v. Smith* (1981), the Court addressed the procedure used by one particular expert in evaluating future dangerousness at sentencing. Dr. James Grigson, a psychiatric expert for the prosecution, had conducted a pretrial evaluation of the defendant's competence to stand trial. He did not inform the defendant prior to that evaluation that the results could be used at sentencing. The Court held that such a notification was necessary, since the Fifth Amendment is applicable to evaluations of capital sentencing and the defendant therefore had a legal right to refuse to answer questions that would adversely affect his position at sentencing. For present purposes, it is Dr. Grigson's approach to evaluating the risk of future criminal violence that is relevant:

**CASE LAW**

*Estelle v. Smith*

● held that defendant must be notified prior to the evaluation if the results of a pretrial evaluation could be used at capital sentencing

Dr. Grigson testified before the jury on direct examination: (a) that Smith "is a very severe sociopath"; (b) that "he will continue his previous behavior"; (c) that his sociopathic condition will "only get worse"; (d) that he has no "regard for another human being's property or for their life, regardless of who it may be"; (e) that "there is no treatment, no medicine . . . that in any way at all modifies or changes this behavior"; (f) that he "is going to go ahead and commit other

similar or same criminal acts if given the opportunity to do so";
and (g) that he "has no remorse or sorrow for what he has
done." (pp. 460–461)

The Court's decision in *Estelle v. Smith* focused on the procedural
aspects of admitting such testimony and how the expert reached his
opinions. In a subsequent decision, however (*Barefoot v. Estelle*,
1983), it was the process for evaluating future risk that was a core
aspect of the U.S. Supreme Court's consideration. There was considerable professional sentiment around this time, exemplified by the
*amicus* brief filed by the American Psychiatric Association in this
case, that mental health professionals had no particular expertise in
predicting violent behavior. In the *Barefoot* context, however, the
Court held that psychiatrists had some expertise in this area that was
no less than the expertise associated with predictions of future
behavior that are often made in other contexts. Such limitations
could be exposed through cross-examination, moreover. While this
opinion should not be mistaken for a ringing endorsement of professional expertise in this context, the Court apparently reasoned
that such testimony provided more advantages than limitations. The
additional consideration in *Barefoot* involved expert testimony in
response to hypothetical questions. Dr. Grigson and another psychiatric expert responded to hypothetical questions rather than obtaining their own information through a direct evaluation. The Court
held this to be legally proper:

> Psychiatric testimony need not be based
> on personal examination of the defendant,
> but may properly be given in response to
> hypothetical questions. Expert testimony,
> whether in the form of an opinion based on
> hypothetical questions or otherwise, is com-
> monly admitted as evidence where it might
> help the factfinder do its job. Although this
> case involves the death penalty, there is no
> constitutional barrier to applying the ordi-
> nary rules of evidence governing the use of
> expert testimony. (pp. 903–904)

**CASE LAW**
*Barefoot v.
Estelle*, 1983

- held that psychiatrists
  had some expertise in
  predicting violent
  behavior

- allowed testimony in
  response to
  hypothetical questions

Two other U.S. Supreme Court cases are relevant. In *Satterwhite v. Texas*, the Court held that the admission of expert psychiatric evidence on future dangerousness at capital sentencing without adequate notice to the defense that the evaluation was being conducted went beyond harmless error, and was not permissible. The Court further held, in *Abdul-Kabir v. Quarterman* (2007), that the trial court's instruction to the jury at sentencing to focus only on the two special issues (whether Cole's conduct was committed deliberately and with the reasonable expectation it would result in his victim's death and whether it was probable he would commit future violent acts constituting a continuing threat to society) and not to consider the potential mitigating impact of evidence beyond these issues, was impermissibly limiting.

There are two important considerations regarding these decisions. First, jurisdiction is very important. All four of these cases come from Texas. The need for (and impact of) violence risk assessment in capital cases is less compelling in other jurisdictions, although it may be important in some cases when considered as a mitigating factor. Second, the influence of context (the defendant's location) is hardly mentioned in these decisions. But an individual who has been convicted of capital murder will probably spend the remainder of his life in prison if he is not executed. Hence, the appropriate context for the prediction is in a highly structured and secure prison. There is a marked difference between risk factors that are applicable in the community versus in prison. Ironically (given the emphasis on the personality disorder of sociopathy and its relation to future violence risk in the cases reviewed in this section), there is strong evidence that psychopathy, a potent risk factor for violent and general offending in the community, does not predict serious violence in secure prison settings (see Cunningham, in press, for a summary of this evidence and a much more detailed discussion of FMHA in capital sentencing contexts).

**INFO**

Texas, unlike most other states, specifically weighs risk of harm to others as part of the capital sentencing process.

## Civil Commitment

The component of civil commitment criteria specifying that an individual must

**CASE LAW**

*Lessard v.
Schmidt* (1973)

● influenced the
  incorporation of a
  "recent overt act" in
  the dangerousness
  component required
  for involuntary civil
  commitment

be "dangerous to self or others" has become far more influential since the 1970s. In *Lessard v. Schmidt* (1973), the U.S. District Court in Eastern District of Wisconsin did not directly address the degree of dangerousness that is constitutionally required for a person to be involuntarily committed. However, the court observed that such involuntary commitment was a "massive curtailment of liberty" that could be justified only when the state could establish an extreme likelihood that if the person is not confined he will do immediate harm to himself or others. Such likelihood should be supported by a finding of a recent overt act, attempt or threat to do substantial harm to oneself or another. This decision influenced subsequent changes to civil commitment statutes in a number of jurisdictions, which incorporated a "recent overt act" requirement in describing how dangerousness should be judged.

The potential impact of living situation on involuntary commitment status was addressed in *O'Connor v. Donaldson* (1975). Rendering a decision on relatively narrow grounds (since Mr. O'Connor had been released from the hospital by the time his case was heard by the U.S. Supreme Court), the Court held that the State cannot constitutionally confine a nondangerous individual who is capable of surviving safely in freedom by himself or with the help of willing and responsible family members or friends. There was some recognition in this decision that an individual who was "nondangerous" in a hospital setting might need assistance from others in maintaining that status in the community—but when such help was available, it was appropriate to assume (through release from hospitalization) that the individual would live safely in the community.

**CASE LAW**

*O'Connor v.
Donaldson* (1975)

● held that the State
  cannot constitutionally
  confine a
  nondangerous
  individual who is
  capable of surviving
  safely in the
  community by himself
  or with the assistance
  of others

## Commitment of Sexually Violent Predators

The decision in *Kansas v. Hendricks* (1997) concerned whether a domain of risk factors for dangerousness to others (Kansas law's definition of "mental abnormality") satisfies substantive due process requirements for individuals who have completed serving a criminal sentence for a sexual offense. The U.S. Supreme Court held that since the Kansas act in question clearly required a finding of dangerousness to self or others prior to post-sentence commitment, and links that finding to a determination that the person suffers from a "mental abnormality" or a "personality disorder," this is legally sufficient. The Court also noted that it had never required States to adopt any particular language in civil commitment statutes, and left to the States the task of defining terms of a medical nature that have legal significance. At least in this context, according to the *Hendricks* decision, if an individual with a personality disorder (defined by a state legislature as a "mental abnormality") was dangerous to self or others as a result of that personality disorder, then that individual could be civilly committed following the completion of the sentence. This decision implicitly speaks to the different standard articulated for "dangerousness" in the context of sexual offending risk. Widespread adoption of the Court's reasoning, if applied to *other* forms of criminal violence, could create statutes allowing post-sentence civil commitment of those at risk for gang violence, armed robbery, and domestic violence (to name but a few) based on their personality disorders.

There does not appear to be any U.S. Supreme Court case law on violence risk assessment in the areas of workplace disability, child custody, or child protection. Case law applicable to juvenile commitment/transfer evaluations is discussed elsewhere in this series (see Andrews & Hoge, in press).

## Legal Procedures

This section addresses two considerations relevant to the procedures involved in any FMHA

**CASE LAW**

*Kansas v. Hendricks* (1997)

● allowed post-sentence commitment of sexually violent predators based on a finding of dangerousness to self or others related to a "mental abnormality" or a "personality disorder" violence risk assessment. It also discusses the steps that are important in this particular kind of forensic assessment.

## Focus on the Referral Question

The first important consideration involves the need to tailor the evaluation specifically to the question(s) raised. Information that is not relevant to the referral questions should be avoided (Melton, Petrila, Poythress, & Slobogin, 2007). This is quite important in evaluating risk for violence. The information gathered in the course of a proper risk assessment can be extensive, but it is clearly sensitive and has the potential for being prejudicial. When the evaluation of violence risk is formally requested in relation to one of the legal issues under consideration, such evaluation should be conducted fully. When it is not, the evaluator should avoid references to risk and risk-relevant needs. It may be, of course, that some of the clinical symptoms and functional-legal capacities evaluated for other kinds of FMHA are also relevant to violence risk and needs. These areas need not be avoided when evaluating other referral questions, but they should *not* be viewed through the lens of risk and risk-relevant needs unless this opinion has been requested specifically.

There are two points at which some evaluators seem tempted to comment on risk without having either focused properly on it or fully evaluated it. Occasionally FMHA reports will contain language that is simply out of place. An evaluator may allude to an individual as "dangerous to self or others" or "likely to reoffend" when that opinion was not formally requested. Evaluators simply must exercise the discipline to describe what they have evaluated and avoid referring to what they have not. The second point can arise during testimony, perhaps upon direct questioning of the expert by the judge. It may be that the need to evaluate risk was not originally conveyed to the expert, even when this information would be relevant to disposition. Under such circumstances, although it may be tempting to be "helpful" to the court, the evaluator should refrain from giving an expert opinion on a question that she has not evaluated.

**BEWARE**
Refrain from giving an opinion on violence of risk either in your report or during testimony when it is not been requested as part of the referral.

## Disclosing Information

The second major consideration involves disclosing information concerning the defendant's functioning that was not the subject of the evaluation. This is particularly applicable in FMHA risk assessment. Information gathered to appraise risk of harm to others may involve areas in which there is legal authority in therapy contexts for breaking therapeutic privilege and disclosing information regarding potential harm to identifiable third parties, abuse of minor children, and (in some jurisdictions) abuse of elders. Valuable guidance in these instances is provided by the ABA *Criminal Justice Mental Health Standards* (1989):

> If in the course of any evaluation, the mental health or mental retardation professional concludes that defendant may be mentally incompetent to stand trial, presents an imminent risk of serious danger to another person, is imminently suicidal, or otherwise needs emergency intervention, the evaluator should notify the defendant's attorney. If the evaluation was initiated by the court or prosecution, the evaluator should also notify the court. (p. 73)

## Steps in Risk Assessment

There are several broad steps associated with FMHA risk assessment. These are steps that are part of any FMHA, but have particular features for risk assessment. (See Figure 1.2).

### REFERRAL AND IDENTIFICATION OF VIOLENCE RISK AS AN ELEMENT

The question of what legal issue(s) will be used to frame the evaluation is the first and most fundamental to be considered. But one specific legal issue does not provide the basis for FMHA risk assessment. For some referral questions, the risk assessment is a contingent aspect of the evaluation. For example, a defendant evaluated for competence to stand trial or mental state at the time of the offense may be described as possibly meeting criteria for involuntary hospitalization (of which violence risk toward others is a part)—but this opinion is provided only when the evaluator's previous conclusion is that the defendant does not appear to meet criteria for competence to stand trial, or appears insane at the time of

## Steps to Risk Assessment

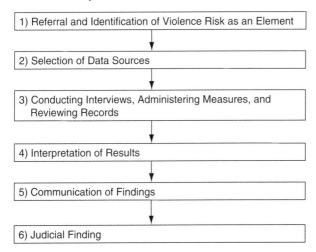

**Figure 1.2**   Steps in Risk Assessment

the offense. For other referral questions, the appraisal of potential harm to others is consistently part of what is being evaluated—but only a part. In the evaluation of civil commitment, for instance, the evaluator would typically consider the nature of the clinical condition and its relation to that individual's risk of harm to self (through active means or grave disability) or others. For yet other referral questions, the risk assessment may address the primary legal issue. When an incarcerated individual is being considered for post-sentence *Hendricks* commitment or community release as a sexual offender, for example, the risk of that individual's reoffending (and perhaps the effectiveness of risk-reducing interventions in this case) is the exclusive basis for the decision. The nature of the referral question in FMHA risk assessment cannot be neatly encapsulated, therefore. But the importance of beginning with the referral question cannot be overstated—particularly since the role of risk assessment in FMHA varies so widely.

## SELECTION OF DATA SOURCES

The conventional sources of information used in FMHA—interview(s) with the individual being evaluated, psychological and

**BEST PRACTICE**
Begin with the referral question when determining the role of risk assessment in the specific FMHA.

specialized testing, and third party information—are also applicable to risk assessment evaluations conducted in legal contexts. The *functional legal capacities* in FMHA risk assessment are the target behaviors (sometimes violence, other times criminal offending more broadly) and their associated risk and protective factors. Accordingly, all information sources will be selected for relevance toward this target behavior and related capacities. This does not mean that the relationship must be direct. In some cases, it can be useful to include a description of symptoms and capacities that are indirectly related to violence risk. Because the risk factors identified by the field as broadly related to violence may not relate as well to the violence risk of an individual, providing a more detailed context for that individual can be helpful. It is also worth noting that violence risk is frequently not the only issue being evaluated in a given FMHA, so the data sources selected will need to be appropriate for all the forensic issues at hand. The selection of data sources is discussed in more detail in Chapter 4.

## CONDUCTING INTERVIEWS, ADMINISTERING MEASURES, AND REVIEWING RECORDS

In addition to selecting particular sources of information, the evaluator must extract a maximal amount of useful information. This can be as straightforward as administering relevant measures just as recommended by the manuals associated with them. Unfortunately, it is often not this simple. There are a variety of challenges to collecting good, risk-relevant information; these include poor testing conditions, sparse or unavailable records, and third party observers who are reluctant to be interviewed. The appearance of exaggeration or minimization in the evaluee's responses calls for the use of a specialized tool to gauge response style carefully. It may also mean that self-reported information cannot be used. These considerations are discussed in more detail in Chapter 5.

## INTERPRETATION OF RESULTS

The interpretation of results necessarily builds on the selection of measures and their use in the context of the challenges of the particular evaluation. Serious problems at either of these two previous stages would substantially limit what can be interpreted. But there is particularly extensive discussion in the field concerning one aspect of risk assessment: When a specialized tool is used, to what extent do the results of this tool contribute to the final conclusion regarding risk? This debate is seen particularly in discussions regarding actuarial assessment, sometimes couched in language such as *adjusted actuarial* assessment. This debate can be misleading. It centers on the question of how a carefully defined outcome can be predicted most accurately. There are many ways in which varying FMHA risk assessments diverge from this question. These, and other interpretive considerations, are discussed in Chapter 6.

## COMMUNICATION OF FINDINGS

Risk assessment performed in legal contexts uses the communication model described for FMHA more generally. This includes providing the sources of information, the resulting data and their interpretation, and the opinions linked to these interpreted data through explicitly described reasoning (Heilbrun et al., 2008; Melton et al., 2007). Expert testimony, when provided, offers a distilled version of the results documented in the report, as well as support for these opinions in the course of cross-examination. Both substantive and stylistic considerations influence the effectiveness of expert testimony (see Brodsky, 1991, 1999, 2004). But there are also considerations specific to FMHA risk assessment, involving the use and approach indicated for sensitive information related to violence risk. These are discussed in more detail in Chapter 7.

## JUDICIAL FINDING

The culmination of the process involving FMHA is the finding made by the legal decision maker. Expert evidence in the form of FMHA risk assessment is only part of the evidence that may be provided. Whether an answer to the ultimate legal question is provided or not, there is little disagreement within the field concerning the importance of providing relevant data that help to inform the court about the relevant functional legal capacities. In FMHA risk assessment, these capacities refer to the individual's risk factors and protective factors—the influences inclining the individual toward and against, respectively, violent behavior. Careful linkage of the factors evaluated with the question before the court can be facilitated by gauging what influences may affect the behavior in question (as noted earlier in the referral and identification steps). It can also lead to a better-informed decision by the court.

# Ethical Considerations in FMHA Risk Assessment

Prediction of future violence is often an important part of FMHA risk assessment. Are such predictions ethical? In a careful analysis of both the empirical evidence and the ethical considerations, Grisso and Appelbaum (1992) offered a qualified "yes" in response to this question. They observed that predictive testimony varies along the ethically relevant dimensions of the nature, foundation, and consequences of the prediction. Much of the previous discussion concerning an ethical ban on predictive testimony centered on predictions made dichotomously (the individual will or will not be dangerous), with little empirical support, in the context of capital sentencing (with severe consequences for false positive predictions) (see Ewing, 1983, 1991). But predictions of violence made in legal contexts address questions that go well beyond the future behavior of those convicted of capital murder. Indeed, the developments in the available empirical evidence and the preferred form of communicating risk since 1992 underscore several of the points made by Grisso and Appelbaum. Risk communication is preferably made in categorical (e.g., low/moderate/high) or frequency (e.g., "1 of 10 such individuals") terms rather than dichotomously, and with empirical support that allows a substantial basis for either statement. Grisso and Appelbaum also predicted that other dimensions would emerge in the discussion of the ethics of risk assessment. They were correct. The dimension of context has become quite important; predictions made about behavior in the community are not necessarily accurate when the individual is incarcerated or in a secure hospital. These points will be discussed in more detail in this book; they will also be addressed in great detail by Cunningham (in press).

## Relevant Ethical Guidance

Consideration of the ethical codes for psychology (*Ethical Principles of Psychologists and Code of Conduct*; American Psychological Association, 2002) and psychiatry (*Principles of Medical Ethics with Annotations Especially Applicable to Psychiatry*; American Psychiatric Association, 2008) provides an important perspective on the current views of these major associations concerning FMHA risk assessment. It is also important to consider the more specialized forensic ethical guidelines for psychology (*Specialty Guidelines for Forensic Psychologists*; Committee on Ethical Guidelines for Forensic Psychologists, 1991) and psychiatry (*Ethics Guidelines for the Practice of Forensic Psychiatry*; AAPL, 2005). There is one important ethical issue that is cited by all four: confidentiality and the limits of confidentiality.

## Confidentiality and the Limits of Confidentialiy

The issue of confidentiality in a forensic context differs from that in a therapy situation. This distinction is clear in the *Principles of Medical Ethics with Annotations Especially Applicable to Psychiatry* (American Psychiatric Association, 2008), which first notes, "A physician shall respect the rights of patients, colleagues, and other health professionals, and shall safeguard patient confidences and privacy within the constraints of the law." It notes a distinction in certain contexts, however:

> Psychiatrists are often asked to examine individuals for security purposes, to determine suitability for various jobs, and to determine legal competence. The psychiatrist must fully describe the nature

**INFO**

Relevant ethical guidance for the forensic clinician include the following:

- *Ethical Principles of Psychologists and Code of Conduct*
- *Principles of Medical Ethics with Annotations Especially Applicable to Psychiatry*
- *Specialty Guidelines for Forensic Psychologists*
- *Ethical Guidelines for the Practice of Forensic Psychiatry*

and purpose and lack of confidentiality of the examination to the examinee at the beginning of the examination. (Section 4, #6)

This distinction is elaborated in the AAPL *Ethical Guidelines*:

> Respect for the individual's right of privacy and the maintenance of confidentiality should be major concerns when performing forensic evaluations. Psychiatrists should maintain confidentiality to the extent possible, given the legal context. Special attention should be paid to the evaluee's understanding of medical confidentiality. A forensic evaluation requires notice to the evaluee and to collateral sources of reasonably anticipated limitations on confidentiality. Information or reports derived from a forensic evaluation are subject to the rules of confidentiality that apply to the particular evaluation, and any disclosure should be restricted accordingly. (Section II)

Both psychiatric authorities emphasize the difference between medical (treatment) confidentiality and that applicable to FMHA. This is consistent with the emphasis on confidentiality noted by the psychology ethics authorities. Under the American Psychological Association's *Ethics Code*, psychologists discuss the limits of confidentiality and the foreseeable uses of the professional product with persons and organizations with whom they have a professional relationship (Standard 4.02). This discussion occurs at the beginning of the relationship, unless "not feasible or contraindicated." The *Specialty Guidelines* both observe that confidentiality in forensic contexts is limited and emphasize that it should be respected when possible:

> Forensic psychologists inform their clients of the limitations to the confidentiality of their services and their products by providing them with an understandable statement of their rights, privileges, and the limitations of confidentiality. (V(B), p. 660)

> In situations where the right of the client or part to confidentiality is limited, the forensic psychologist makes every effort to maintain confidentiality with regard to any information that does not bear directly upon the legal purpose of the evaluation. (V(C), p. 660)

**BEST PRACTICE**

Notify individuals of the limits of confidentiality and respect confidentiality when possible.

It seems clear that the limits of confidentiality are closely related to the purpose for which the evaluation is being conducted. In FMHA risk assessment, as in other kinds of forensic assessments, the referral questions are provided to the evaluee in the notification given prior to starting the evaluation. Within the limits of those referral questions, and with parties formally involved in the litigation, the concept of "confidentiality" is secondary to relevant evidentiary law. For extra-litigation purposes, however, confidentiality and its ethical boundaries are an important influence of what is disclosed, and to whom.

## Conclusion

This chapter has addressed the legal contexts and precedents applicable to evaluations of violence risk that are conducted as part of litigation. Many risk assessments are conducted for reasons unrelated to litigation; these are distinguished in the present book from evaluations performed in forensic contexts. There are also a number of topics addressed by other authors in this series that focus on a specific kind of risk assessment. This book, by contrast, will address the contours of risk assessment specifically within FMHA—but broadly enough to cover the aspects of risk assessment applicable to differing legal questions. The next step will involve discussing forensic mental health concepts, to which we now turn in Chapter 2.

# Forensic Mental Health Concepts

# 2

Forensic mental health concepts, which have also been called functional legal capacities, are at the heart of FMHA. Models of the forensic assessment process consistently cite such functional legal capacities as essential elements of evaluations for the courts (see Grisso, 2003; Morse, 1978 for examples of such models). Therefore, to address best practice in any given FMHA, it is important to describe the functional legal capacities that are a part of that particular FMHA and indicate how they will be assessed.

This chapter addresses such forensic mental health concepts for FMHA risk assessment. The focus in this book is upon risk assessment broadly, however. Therefore, this description of risk assessment must be sufficiently broad to encompass the range of different risk assessments performed in legal contexts. The chapter begins by describing important contours of risk assessment that need to be considered: context, purpose, population, parameters, and approach. Ideally these considerations are made clear through relevant statutes, case law, and the nature of the legal authorization. Often they are not. Accordingly, this chapter describes strategies for addressing general and/or unelaborated FMHA legal standards in the course of risk assessment evaluations. The chapter concludes with 10 principles of FMHA risk assessment, with associated implications for the forensic clinician who conducts such evaluations.

**INFO**

Considerations for FMHA risk assessment:

- Context
- Purpose
- Population
- Parameters
- Approach

## Important Aspects of Risk Assessment Not Necessarily Addressed in the Referral Question

The practice of FMHA risk assessment in some respects might be analogized to the practice of evaluating legal competencies. Clearly there are common elements and procedures; just as clearly, there are respects in which such evaluations differ. Grisso (2003) constructed a framework within which the measures for different legal competencies could be critically analyzed. This section will take a similar approach. Discussion of FMHA risk assessment, with the common and disparate elements of different kinds of evaluations, can be informed by the consideration of context, purpose, population, parameters, and approach (Heilbrun, Yasuhara, & Shah, in press).

### Context

The first consideration in FMHA risk assessment is the context in which it is being conducted. Context helps to identify the nature of the decision, the decision maker, and the decision's consequences. There are four different contexts in which a risk assessment may be performed: legal, clinical, school/workplace, and threats to protectees. This book focuses on the first, but it is important to recognize all four.

*Legal contexts* involve having a legal decision maker render a decision in the course of litigation, which include criminal, civil, or child/family proceedings. Legal decisions involving violence risk components may include initial commitment or sentencing, release from incarceration or secure hospitalization, or steps associated with a planned release.

*Clinical contexts* involve risk reduction interventions provided in the course of treatment. These interventions may be delivered in secure settings (e.g., correctional and forensic facilities) or in other contexts associated with some

**INFO**

A risk assessment may be conducted in four different contexts:

1. Legal
2. Clinical
3. School/workplace
4. Threats to protectees

leverage (e.g., for individuals diverted from prosecution, or those on parole or probation). They may also be provided on a fully voluntary basis, such as psychotherapy in a jurisdiction with a legal obligation on the therapist to warn or protect identifiable third parties from patient violence.

*School contexts* and *workplace contexts* include threats and aggression toward others that are usually outside the scope of legal proceedings. These risk assessments usually focus on an individual and are initiated by concerns suggesting the possibility of serious harm toward others in the school or workplace setting.

Finally, *threats to protectees* involve both threat assessment and risk management. However, they differ from other contexts because they involve targets who are protected by a particular agency (e.g., the Secret Service or U.S. Marshals Service), those involved in domestic situations in which the police are called to intervene, or targets associated with domestic or international terrorism.

This range of contexts demonstrates how risk assessment applies well beyond the present legal focus. Perspectives on particular problems outside the scope of this book are available for matters such as school violence (see, e.g., Cornell, 2003, 2006), stalking (see, e.g., Meloy, 1998, 2000), threat assessment in a *Tarasoff* context (see, e.g., Borum & Reddy, 2001), and inpatient violence (see, e.g., McNiel & Binder, 1994; Richter & Whittington, 2006).

## Purpose

The transition from "dangerousness" to "risk assessment" facilitated greater precision and applicability in describing influences in risk factor domains (Kraemer et al., 1997; Monahan & Steadman, 1994). The risk/needs/responsivity (RNR) model (Andrews & Bonta, 2006; Andrews, Bonta, & Hoge, 1990; Andrews, Bonta, & Wormith, 2006) has also influenced some contemporary approaches to risk assessment. It has its roots in approaches to evaluating and rehabilitating offenders, but has clearly also influenced FMHA risk assessment in its specification of three related domains. *Risk* refers to the probability that the examinee will engage in violence, offending, or the specified target behavior; higher-risk individuals are theorized to need more intensive intervention and management services. This domain is measured by both *prediction-oriented* and *risk-needs* tools; the distinction depends on whether the tool is designed only to offer the most accurate appraisal of the individual's likelihood of behaving in the targeted way, or intended to address both risk level and risk-relevant needs. Such *needs* are deficits related to the probability of targeted outcomes. They are composed of dynamic risk factors (*criminogenic needs* in the RNR model) and/or protective factors. For either type, factors must have the potential to change through planned intervention in order to be relevant in the RNR model. *Responsivity* is the extent to which an individual is likely to respond favorably to intervention(s) delivered with the goal of reducing the probability of the targeted outcome behavior.

Heilbrun (1997) made a similar distinction involving FMHA risk assessment, noting the difference between prediction and risk management. Some legal decisions are best informed by a prediction of whether the target behavior will occur. An example of such a decision is post-sentence *Hendricks* commitment for sexual offenders (see Witt & Conroy, 2008, for a fuller discussion). The decision depends almost exclusively upon the question of the individual's likelihood of reoffending sexually if released to the community; higher-risk offenders are more likely to be committed than lower-risk offenders. There is no apparent risk management component to this decision if the sentencing court will not retain jurisdiction over those who are committed to decide when they are sufficiently "low risk" for release into the community. However, when the court maintains jurisdiction over the defendant (e.g., when the case is diverted to mental health court), then both level of risk and the nature of the risk-relevant needs are important components of the court's decision.

**INFO**

Prediction and risk management are two different components of risk assessment; one may be better suited to the legal question at hand than the other.

## Populations

The population or subpopulation to which the individual being assessed belongs is also important for several

**INFO**

The following factors are often used to distinguish populations:

- Age
- Gender
- Mental health status
- Location

reasons. Different groups may have distinctive (a) base rates of violence or offending, (b) risk factors and protective factors, and (c) risk-relevant interventions and management strategies. Specialized tools incorporate such base rates, risk/protective factors, and (sometimes) intervention needs, so usually they are derived and validated on a single population (e.g., adults with severe mental illness but without criminal involvement in the community) or related populations (e.g., adult offenders), but not across populations that differ substantially.

What is a reasonable way to consider how populations differ? Four dimensions—age, gender, mental health status, and location—appear relevant. *Age* is used to distinguish preadolescent children, adolescents, and adults; these groups differ in a variety of respects relevant to violence. Base rates of violence also differ by *gender* in some contexts, so this is always an important variable to consider. A specialized tool that has been validated on only those of one gender cannot, in the absence of empirical evidence, be used in evaluating those of the other gender. *Mental health status* describes the extent to which individuals are selected for a population because of mental health problems. For present purposes, such specific selection might also include substance abuse problems identified as separate or as co-occurring disorders. Finally, *location* refers to the setting from which the population is drawn, with community versus incarceration (correctional facility, secure hospital) an important distinction. The challenges in risk assessment intensify when the evaluation appraises the risk of the target behavior in a setting different than the individual's current setting—for instance, when individuals in a secure setting under *Hendricks* commitment are considered for their risk of sexual violence in the community following release. Consideration of all four of these variables informs the evaluator's decision about whether a given individual is sufficiently similar to the population on which a given specialized risk assessment tool was validated to justify using that tool as part of the specific evaluation.

Another dimension, that of racial/ethnic group, is also important, although in a somewhat different way. The dimensions of age, gender, mental health status, and location can be considered primary determinants in the selection of a specialized risk assessment measure. That is, it may be entirely inappropriate to use a specialized measure developed on one subgroup (e.g., adolescents) with another subgroup (adults). Racial/ethnic status does not appear to be a primary determinant for the selection of a specialized tool in the same way. The goal is not to develop one specialized tool for African Americans, another for Hispanics, and a third for whites. Instead, it is important (if a risk assessment tool is to be used for an individual in one of these groups) to demonstrate that a given risk assessment tool has been validated for use with individuals within the same racial/ethnic group as the individual being evaluated. In addition, evaluators should attend to the empirical research evidence on the limits of applicability of a certain specialized tool with a particular racial/ethnic group, even if the tool is selected. For instance, there is evidence (see, e.g., Fass, Heilbrun, DeMatteo, & Fretz, 2008) that African American inmates tend to be overclassified (substantial false positive rates in predicting reoffending) when assessed using general criminogenic risk factors or either of two specialized risk assessment measures—the LSI-R (Andrews & Bonta, 2001) or the COMPAS (Brennan & Oliver, 2000). When there is no available empirical evidence concerning the applicability of a specialized risk assessment tool to individuals in a given racial/ethnic group, then best practice would suggest that the tool not be used with individuals in this particular group.

## Parameters

There are a number of additional considerations that help to refine the specificity of the risk assessment task. These will be considered as follows: target behavior, frequency, probability/risk category, setting(s), outcome period, and risk and protective factors.

Specification of the target behavior being predicted is quite important. It is relevant to the base rate (broad classes of behavior

**INFO**

Parameters to be considered in relation to risk include the following:

- Target behavior
- Frequency
- Probability/risk category
- Setting(s)
- Outcome period
- Risk and protective factors

**2**
chapter

such as minor aggression have relatively high base rates; narrow classes of behavior such as serial homicide have extremely low base rates) and the degree of concordance with the legal question. How target behavior outcomes will be measured is another important question. If an individual being considered for release from *Hendricks* commitment into the community is arrested for shoplifting, is that to be counted among the target behaviors for which risk is being appraised? If that same individual, following release to the community, is found in possession of magazines such as *Playboy* or *Penthouse*, is that among the target behaviors? The complexity increases when there are behavioral outcomes that are considerably different from the typical outcomes for violence that are used in research studies. Frequent sources used to contribute to measuring violence outcomes include (a) self-report, (b) collateral observer report, and (c) official records (e.g., rearrest, rehospitalization). One large research study with individuals in the community, hospitalized for psychiatric reasons but without formal criminal involvement, suggests that the most sensitive of these three measures is self-report, followed by collateral observation, with official records a relatively insensitive measure of whether violence has occurred (Monahan et al., 2001; Steadman et al., 1998). But this study used behavior, and not alleged offending, as its primary measure of violence outcome. This may differ from the outcome that applies in a given FMHA risk assessment, in which the individual in a forensic context may have a much stronger incentive to deny or minimize self-reported violent behavior.

The specific aspects of the target behavior are also important: Do they include serious violence only? Must this behavior result in a criminal arrest or conviction? Is less serious aggression included? Does the legal question focus on a specific kind of violence (e.g., domestic violence)? Are verbal threats included? Is a single act sufficient to reflect the occurrence of the designated outcome, or are multiple acts necessary? (Often multiple acts cannot be recorded, since a single act of sufficient seriousness will usually result in reincarceration or more intensive monitoring that changes the nature of the risk.) Over what period of time is the appraisal focused? (Such outcome periods can range from extremely short— perhaps as short as 24 hours in some cases—to extending over periods as long as 5–10 years. Outcome periods of 6–12 months began to be used more often in research conducted in the 1980s and later; it is now less frequent that extremely long outcomes are used in developing and validating specialized risk assessment tools.)

Location is also important. The risk of violent behavior in a structured setting such as a secure juvenile facility, prison, or secure hospital is different from the risk in the community when the evaluee is released, for a variety of reasons. Greater structure means more intensive observation by and interaction with staff members, the absence of drugs, alcohol, and weapons, more rules, greater chance of being detected in violating rules, and the provision of relevant medical and nonmedical treatment. Outside a structured setting, the individual may be in a range of environments with differing influences, such as home, work, school, and a variety of public settings. Targets for violence may be much more accessible. There may be more factors that limit compliance with treatment, and noncompliance is more likely to be undetected. These situational aspects of violence risk have been studied less than the contributions of personal influences (Steadman, 1982), but there are more recent examples of research considering the influence of neighborhood (Silver, 2001), hospital (Ogloff & Daffern, 2006), and prison (Cooke, Wozniak, & Johnstone, 2008) settings on violence risk.

Finally, it is important for evaluators to describe the basis for their conclusions regarding risk level and needs. Some structured professional judgment tools may help accomplish this by identifying the risk factors, protective factors, and broader domains within which these factors fall. It may be more challenging with actuarial risk assessment tools, which select predictors for their empirical relationship to outcome rather than their theoretical or commonsense relationship.

## Approach

Three approaches in risk assessment using specialized tools will be described in this book: *actuarial, structured professional judgment,* and *anamnestic.* The use of unstructured clinical judgment will be discussed only briefly as a predictive approach, as there is an extensive history of research demonstrating that it is consistently, albeit modestly, less accurate than actuarial approaches. However, in FMHA risk assessment, "clinical judgment" does have an important part to play. It can help to shape the interviews of the evaluee and collaterals, interpret input from records, guide the integration of materials from multiple sources, and reason toward conclusions. A much more extensive discussion of clinical judgment, and a comparison of the actuarial, structured professional judgment, and anamnestic approaches to risk assessment, is presented in the next chapter.

## Applicability

How applicable is a given specialized risk assessment tool to a particular case? How congruent are the nature of the evaluation and the attributes of the specialized tool? Such congruence can be gauged by considerations such as context, purpose, populations, and parameters. The information needed to make this decision should be included in the manual of the specialized tool, underscoring the importance of having such a manual (Heilbrun, Rogers, & Otto, 2002). The issue of congruence, and the decision whether to use a given tool, can become more complex when the context of the legal question is not very similar to that described in the tool's manual.

# Strategy for Addressing FMHA Legal Standards That Are General and Unelaborated

It is often the case that the referral question in FMHA risk assessment will not address all of the parameters described in the previous section. Indeed, it would be extremely unusual for each of these to be clear in a given evaluation. Considering this, how ought the evaluator to proceed?

It should first be recognized that "unelaborated legal standards"—particularly the use of the words "dangerous" and "dangerousness"—were a substantial reason why medical and behavioral science moved from using these terms to using "risk assessment." "Dangerousness" as a concept cannot be easily disaggregated. "Risk assessment," by contrast, immediately raises questions concerning risk level, nature of the outcome, and contributing risk factors and protective factors (National Research Council, 1989). But the legal concept of dangerousness and the professional/scientific view of risk assessment may not be synonymous, even when the components of the risk assessment and the embedded assumptions are described clearly in the legal standards.

The strategy that has generally been used in FMHA in the face of legal standards that are insufficiently specific is as follows: (a) the functional legal capacities (rather than the ultimate legal question) are the focus; (b) the assumptions and definitions used in the evaluation are made clear; and (c) if there is a range of potential outcome severity that is unspecified, different opinions are provided for different outcomes of interest (Heilbrun, 2001). In legal contexts, "dangerousness" is often treated as a dichotomous variable—the individual is or is not dangerous. Such dichotomies should be avoided in the report. The preferable emphasis for risk level is communicated using probabilities or multiple risk levels. However, such a dichotomy can be more difficult to avoid in cross-examination if the evaluator is asked, "Doctor, is this man dangerous? Yes or no?" One of the most useful responses to this question is, "It depends." It is responsive to the question but obviously incomplete. When the evaluator is able to talk about the considerations on which it depends, then they become easier to specify and the misleading dichotomy easier to avoid.

**BEST PRACTICE**

FMHA STRATEGY FOR INSUFFICIENTLY SPECIFIC LEGAL STANDARDS:

1. Focus on the functional legal capacities (rather than the ultimate legal question).

2. Clarify the assumptions and definitions used in the evaluation.

3. Provide different outcomes of interest if there is an unspecified range of potential outcome severity.

# Principles of Risk Assessment

There are 10 principles of FMHA risk assessment that are helpful in specifying the functional legal capacities that are at the heart of FMHA risk assessment. These principles and their implications for best practice are discussed next (see Table 2.1).

**Table 2.1** Principles of Risk Assessment and Implications for Best Practice

| Principles of Risk Assessment | Implications for Best Practice |
|---|---|
| Identification of the Task | Identify Whether Assessment of Risk-Relevant Needs Is Required in Addition to Prediction |
| Specification of the Context | Specify the Setting in Which the Risk of the Target Behavior Is Being Appraised (e.g., Residential vs. Community) |
| Specification of Outcome | Clarify the Outcome(s) for Which Risk is Being Assessed and Consider Outcome Specification at Every Stage of the Evaluation |
| Identification of the Population | Match the Use of Specialized Risk Assessment Tool(s) with the Population to Which the Evaluee Belongs |
| Estimate of Base Rate | Consider Base Rates of the Specific Outcome(s) for the Population to Which the Evaluee Belongs |
| Identification of Risk Factors and Protective factors | Describe the Factors that Contribute to Future Risk of the Target Behavior |
| Individualization of Assessment | Use both Nomothetic an.d Idiographic Approaches |

*(Continued)*

| Principles of Risk Assessment | Implications for Best Practice |
|---|---|
| Communication of Risk in Probability, Frequency, or Relative Terms | Express Risk with Probability- or Frequencies-Based Statements When Using Actuarial Tools, but Only with Terms of Relative Risk When Using Structured Professional Judgment (SPJ) |
| Description of Risk-Relevant Needs | When Indicated by the Referral Question, Assess Risk-Relevant Needs Through the Use of a Specialized Tool or other Means |
| Impact of Values if the Ultimate Legal Question is Answered | If Answering the Ultimate Legal Question, Acknowledge the Role of Personal Values in Determining "Dangerousness" |

## Identification of the Task

The FMHA risk assessment referral question typically calls for an appraisal of the future risk of a specific type of behavior. But does the risk assessment question also call for an assessment of risk-relevant needs? The answer to this question will affect the entire evaluation, from conceptualization to data source selection (particularly the choice of a specialized risk assessment tool) to communication of results and conclusions in the report and testimony.

## Specification of the Context

In what setting is the risk of the target behavior being appraised? There are substantial differences between community and residential settings that affect the risk assessment process. If the assessment involves evaluating an individual in one context (e.g., a secure hospital) for risk in another context (e.g., on conditional release in the community), then the task becomes more complex. A clear description of the individual's current and future environments (including aspects such as living circumstances, work, treatment, social support, monitoring, and other important situational features) is quite important, and it is consistent with best practice in this area.

## Specification of Outcome

Clarity about the outcome(s) for which risk is assessed is essential. Substantial differences in the base rates of different kinds of violent or antisocial behavior often exist, with less serious aggression generally more prevalent (but often of less interest to the decision maker). There are a number of relevant questions concerning the outcome: How specific is it? Does it focus on a particular kind of offending (e.g., sexual offending, domestic violence), or would any offense against persons count? Must the aggression be relatively serious, or is more minor aggression included? (The MacArthur Research Network distinguished between serious acts of violence and other aggressive acts, with the former defined by behavior resulting in harm to another person or a threat with a weapon in hand. They demonstrated that rates of occurrence and risk factors differed substantially between these two classes of outcome; see Monahan et al., 2001.) Over what period of time is the risk of this outcome to be appraised? Is a single occurrence of the behavior sufficient, or is frequency a consideration? Is the target behavior domain broad enough to encompass any criminal offending whatsoever? Specialized risk assessment tools are derived and validated against specific outcomes, so when such a tool is used it is important to indicate that the results reflect a level of risk *for a certain kind of outcome behavior.* Outcome specification is important at every stage throughout the evaluation, from initial conceptualization through communication of risk in the form of conclusions and opinions.

## Identification of the Population

The parameters of risk assessment for one population do not necessarily generalize to a different population. Certainly the use of a specialized risk assessment tool in a population different than that on which it was derived and validated, or for which there is empirical evidence regarding its effectiveness, is not indicated.

## Estimate of Base Rate

The specification of target behavior and population allows an evaluator to investigate the available evidence on base rates of this kind of outcome within this population. This investigation can be a laborious task; it is less essential if the evaluator uses a specialized risk assessment tool which includes the base rates of outcome as part of the process of interpreting the results. But there is no question regarding the importance of such base rates to the risk assessment process. Nearly 30 years ago, Monahan (1981) identified ignorance of base rates of the outcome as one of the most serious shortcomings associated with violence risk assessment.

## Identification of Risk Factors and Protective Factors

It is important for the evaluator to provide a reasonably accurate appraisal of the risk of future violence, and (if this is part of the task) to describe risk-relevant needs. Even when such needs appraisal is not part of the FMHA risk assessment, however, it is useful for the evaluator to be able to explain some of the aspects of the individual's functioning that contribute to future risk. In actuarial assessment, there need not be a direct relationship between enumerated risk factors and the conclusion about risk level—it is a question of which risk factors are most strongly related to outcome, and the statistical nature of that relationship. Structured professional judgment differs from actuarial prediction in this respect. With SPJ, the evaluator's conclusion is made through consideration of various risk factors and protective factors; therefore, identification and description of these factors is crucial in using SPJ tools.

## Individualization of Assessment

There is a constant tension in FMHA between the use of measures that are developed nomothetically (group-referenced, using conventional scientific research designs) and approaches that are idiographic (individually referenced, using the evaluee's own history of functioning and behavior). The development of specialized measures in FMHA has yielded a substantially stronger empirical foundation for the field. Yet the law seeks individualized justice; to advocate the application of a specialized measure in FMHA without also obtaining a good deal of information specifically about the individual would risk substituting behavioral science values for legal priorities. The resolution consistent with best practice involves using both approaches. Individualized information can be obtained in risk assessment through detailed questioning of the evaluee about current and historical thoughts, feelings, motivations, fantasies, and behavior relevant to violence. This is discussed in more detail in the next chapter under "Anamnestic Assessment."

This individualized approach can yield substantively valuable information. It also increases the face validity of the risk assessment, a very important consideration in FMHA (Grisso, 2003). This point is perhaps best illustrated by imagining its absence. What would a court or a jury think of an evaluation that did not include direct questioning of the individual regarding such information? How would an evaluator explain the failure to directly question the individual regarding violent behavior, thoughts, and feelings, as recommended by Monahan (1993), with respect to *Tarasoff* liability?

## Communication of Risk in Probability, Frequency, or Relative Terms

When risk is conveyed in terms of probabilities or ordinal categories, this is particularly informative. But there is an important distinction between actuarial measures and structured professional judgment tools that is relevant to this discussion. A good, well-developed actuarial measure can provide an association between score and outcome frequency that allows statements phrased in probability terms ("Mr. Jones is 10% likely to commit a serious act of violence over the next 6 months") or frequencies ("1 of 10 individuals with a score like that of Mr. Jones will commit a serious act of violence over the next 6 months"). Using a structured professional judgment tool, however, the evaluator draws a conclusion about risk from considering the presence of risk factors and protective factors. The relative accuracy of each approach is discussed in the next chapter. But it should be clear that the SPJ tool does not provide a basis for either a probability- or a frequencies-based statement about risk. Rather, the conclusion is expressed in terms of relative risk—the individual with a substantial history of violence and numerous risk factors will be rated as a relatively higher risk than will the individual with a modest history of violence and fewer risk factors. But there are no precise quantitative aspects to such a conclusion, as these are not available using the SPJ tool.

## Description of Risk-Relevant Needs

When FMHA risk assessment calls for a prediction only, there is no point in describing the needs that exacerbate an individual's risk. This underscores the importance of identifying the task. If needs appraisal, and perhaps recommendation or planning for interventions, is part of the evaluation, then the evaluator must either incorporate a risk-needs tool (if available) or make plans to assess risk-relevant needs in alternative ways.

## Impact of Values If the Ultimate Legal Question Is Answered

There are personal values that enter into any opinion that directly answers the ultimate legal question. The more limited the specification of included parameters, the greater the potential influence of such personal values. There are apparently no empirical data on clinicians' views on the question of "how likely is too likely?" Judges' values have been described in only one study (see Monahan & Silver, 2003). Consider, for instance, the individual who has been identified through FMHA risk assessment, including a specialized actuarial tool, as "10% likely to commit a serious act of violence during the next 6 months, with a 95% confidence interval for this estimate of 8–12%." Is this person dangerous? This is a question the author has routinely asked audiences in the risk assessment workshops he has conducted over the last 18 years. Some audiences have been almost entirely composed of psychologists. Others have been mixed, and have included judges, attorneys, physicians, nurses, social workers, parole and probation officers, case workers, and ward staff members. The pattern of responses is striking—there is no pattern. Some individuals will respond "yes" to the question of whether this "10% likely" individual is dangerous. The majority of the audience typically raises a hand by the time we reach "50% likely." There have been a few who do not respond affirmatively until we reach "90% likely." As diverse as these responses are, they come from a group that is relatively homogeneous when compared with the cross section of citizens that may compose a jury. It seems likely that the use of the term "dangerous" permits a very substantial role for the influence of personal values. If the evaluator decides to respond to this question, he should add that his answer is affected not only by the appraised level of risk, but also by his own values that help to define the level of risk necessary for an individual to be considered dangerous.

## Conclusions

This chapter has addressed the forensic mental health concepts associated with a wide range of risk assessments conducted in legal contexts. Given this range, the focus was upon broader parameters rather than the specific aspects of any particular kind of risk assessment. The role of specialized risk assessment tools played a prominent part in this discussion. These tools have been instrumental in advancing the accuracy and forensic utility of various kinds of risk assessment. As such, they are the FMHA components about which it is most meaningful to discuss "empirical foundations and limits." It is to that topic that we turn in the next chapter.

# Empirical Foundations and Limits | 3

T his chapter will address the empirical foundations and limitations of several different approaches to risk assessment. The discussion will focus particularly on specialized risk assessment tools of two kinds: *actuarial* and *structured professional judgment* (*SPJ*), both of which can be described as structured risk assessment (Monahan, 2008). A third approach to risk assessment, termed *anamnestic*, will also be discussed. This is an analytic approach that is less amenable to empirical study, so there is little to describe with respect to empirical foundations. However, for reasons described in this chapter, it is an important aspect of FMHA risk assessment.

Accordingly, this chapter will focus on the approaches of actuarial and SPJ approaches to risk assessment, as these are the areas in which it is most meaningful to discuss empirical foundations. They are supported by relevant research. Some of this research compares these two approaches. There is also a long standing history of research demonstrating the value of actuarial approaches to prediction of various target behaviors. In this context, these two approaches will be discussed, with additional comments concerning the nature and role of anamnestic assessment.

Following the discussion of the empirical foundations of actuarial and SPJ approaches, this chapter will describe four specialized risk assessment tools. These were selected because each is an established measure, and is reasonably consistent with the criteria for a good measure in forensic contexts (proposed by Heilbrun, Rogers, & Otto, 2002) at the same time consistent with the current notion of best practice: commercial publication, available test manual, demonstrated levels of reliability and validity, successful peer review, and decision-making formulas known to the examiner. Examples of measures that are *actuarial* and *prediction oriented* (the VRAG; Harris, Rice, & Quinsey, 1993; and the COVR; Monahan, Steadman, Appelbaum et al., 2005), *actuarial* and *risk needs* (the LS/CMI; Andrews, Bonta, & Wormith, 2004), and *SPJ* and *risk needs* (the HCR-20; Webster, Douglas, Eaves, & Hart, 1997) will be discussed. This will demonstrate the empirical foundations and limitations of these four widely accepted risk assessment tools. It will also model an approach to considering the strengths and limitations of other specialized tools.

First, however, it is useful to offer some brief comments about the use of unstructured clinical judgment.

## Unstructured Clinical Judgment

The use of unstructured clinical judgment in risk assessment will not be evaluated in detail in this chapter. There are several reasons for this. First, when "unstructured clinical judgment" is defined as the evaluator's judgment about risk unaided by additional materials— basically a "free-form" approach to risk assessment—this approach does not fare well when compared with actuarial assessment in accuracy of predictions of violence. There is a history of research spanning over 50 years comparing the accuracy of unstructured clinical judgment with actuarial approaches on a variety of questions. Such research has yielded a consistent (albeit modest) advantage in predictive accuracy observed for actuarial approaches (see Ægosdóttir et al., 2006, and Grove, Zald, Lebow, Snitz, & Nelson, 2000, for relevant meta-analyses). In the violence prediction domain, another meta-analysis (Mossman, 1994) noted that clinical predictions were more accurate than chance ($AUC = .67$) but less accurate than the mean $AUC$ (area under the curve) for all studies (.78), for cross-validated discriminant function predictions (.71), or for behavior-based predictions (.78). Second, it is important to distinguish unstructured clinical judgment as it would be applied to making a prediction or assessing risk-relevant needs (where greater structure clearly seems to improve both tasks) from the clinical judgment that is necessary throughout various aspects of FMHA risk assessment. Such aspects include the selection of sources, the administration and interpretation of various measures and other sources, and the linkage of data with opinions through clearly described reasoning. In all of these respects, the evaluator's judgment provides a very important contribution. But the selection, administration, and interpretation aspects of FMHA risk assessment are

particularly enhanced by using specialized risk assessment tools and analytic, structured approaches to interviewing—and the use of such tools and analytic strategies is consistent with best practice in contemporary FMHA risk assessment. Third, unstructured clinical judgment alone is consequently neither an adequate nor a useful approach to appraising violence risk at present. If a specialized risk assessment tool is not available in a particular case, then best practice would suggest that evaluators should "structure" their risk appraisals by focusing on known risk factors and protective factors for the target outcome, with such factors identified through the research literature, the individual's history, or both.

**3**
chapter

# Types of Assessment Approaches

## Actuarial Assessment

Actuarial assessment is "a formal method" that "uses an equation, a formula, a graph, or an actuarial table to arrive at a probability, or expected value, of some outcome" (Grove & Meehl, 1996, p. 294). It uses quantified predictor variables which are validated through empirical research, focusing on the outcome of interest (which must also be quantified). The predictors and weights are typically obtained through empirical research as well. This could involve a single (hopefully large) data set gathered by the researcher, or multiple data sets combined through meta-analytic techniques. So the central defining feature of actuarial assessment entails using an objective, mechanistic, reproducible combination of predictive factors, selected and validated through empirical research against known outcomes.

**INFO**
Useful approaches to risk assessment:

● Actuarial assessment
● Structured professional judgment
● Anamnestic assessment

## Structured Professional Judgment

SPJ uses specified risk factors that are not necessarily obtained from a particular data set. Indeed, the SPJ tools currently available have identified their risk and protective factors from a review of the literature. Once selected, these items must be carefully operationalized, so that their presence can be reliably coded. Evaluators using an SPJ tool consider various sources of information (interviews, records, and other sources of information) in rating the presence of the specified items. Following this, evaluators weigh the presence of the risk factors and the anticipated intensity of management, treatment, or supervision needs in drawing a conclusion about the individual's risk. This conclusion is a matter of professional judgment, structured by the requirement that the evaluator consider relevant information and rate the tool's items. But these items are not scored and combined to yield a "total score," as is typically done in actuarial assessment. Thus, SPJ is more flexible but less precise than actuarial assessment. SPJ allows greater flexibility because the evaluator can consider influences beyond the specified items in making a judgment. It is less precise because the evaluator has no basis for providing an estimate of the quantitative meaning of "low risk" or "high risk"—as is possible with an actuarial tool. How these two types of tools compare will be addressed further in this chapter.

 **INFO**

Similarities and Differences Between Actuarial and SPJ Procedures

Actuarial and SPJ procedures are actually similar in a number of respects. Both use risk factors and protective factors selected for their empirical relationship to the target outcome. Both specify the variables to be considered on the particular tool. Both require these variables be operationalized to allow reliability in rating. However, they also differ in several other respects. The most important of these is the way in which the final judgment regarding risk is reached. Actuarial approaches use a total score that is associated with an identified frequency of occurrence of the target outcome; SPJ measures leave the final judgment to the evaluator, although requiring that the relevant information and rated items on the tool be reviewed in drawing this conclusion concerning risk.

## Anamnestic Assessment

The third approach might better be characterized as a process than a specialized tool. Anamnestic assessment (Melton, Petrila, Poythress, & Slobogin, 2007) is an approach

**BEWARE**
Anamnestic assessment by itself is not sufficient for predicting future behavior or rating risk relative to others.

that can provide a useful complement to the information provided by specialized tools, and is also useful in the process of "individualizing" the assessment. This approach uses applied behavior analytic strategies, seeking detailed information from an individual regarding previous behavior that is similar to the target outcome. The evaluee is asked detailed questions regarding such prior acts, including preceding and subsequent thoughts, feelings, and behaviors, the act itself, those involved, and relevant details (e.g., whether drugs or alcohol were ingested, by whom, and at what level; whether weapons were involved, and their source; how victim(s) were targeted, where and when the event occurred, and other relevant details). This is a pattern-detection process. The evaluator seeks to identify recurring themes across different acts, including commonalities of personal and situational variables. When a pattern or recurring theme is observed, this forms the basis for a risk factor (or protective factor) derived from "the individual's own history" rather than being taken from broader risk factors applicable to the violent behavior of many. The strength of anamnestic assessment involves the identification of risk factors and the gauging of patterns that are directly applicable to the individual being evaluated. It also points to dynamic risk factors that can serve as targets for intervention, reducing that individual's risk of violence if the intervention is successful. It does not, however, provide a good basis for a prediction of future behavior or the relative rating of risk.

## Actuarial and Structured Professional Judgment Approaches to Risk Assessment: Empirical Foundations

This section will cover the available empirical evidence relevant to actuarial and SPJ approaches to risk assessment considered separately. It will also describe studies in which the two approaches are compared. Finally, it will provide a description of the empirical foundations (and limitations) for anamnestic assessment.

## Actuarial Approaches

There have been a number of meta-analyses in this area. Bonta, Law, and Hanson (1998) focused on studies of mentally disordered offenders using the outcomes of general offending (any kind of rearrest or reconviction) and violent reoffending (involving crimes against persons). A number of predictors were identified which could potentially be incorporated into an actuarial assessment measure (see Table 3.1).

### PSYCHOPATHY AND RISK ASSESSMENT TOOLS

The variable of psychopathy has been consistently associated with violent offending in the community over a number of studies.

**Table 3.1** | Predictors of Violent Recidivism (Bonta et al., 1998)

| Positive Predictors | |
|---|---|
| • Objective Risk Assessment (With the Largest Recidivism Effect Size of .30), | • Hospital Admissions |
| • Adult Criminal History | • Substance Abuse |
| • Juvenile Delinquency | • Family Problems |
| • Antisocial Personality Disorder | • Violent History |
| • Nonviolent Criminal History | • Single Marital Status |
| • Institutional Adjustment | |
| **Negative Predictors** | |
| • Mentally Disordered Offender Status | • Not Guilty by Reason of Insanity |
| • Age | • Psychosis |

One measure of psychopathy, the Psychopathy Checklist-Revised (PCL-R; Hare, 1991), was compared using meta-analysis (Gendreau, Goggin, & Smith, 2002) with the predictive performance of the Level of Service Inventory-Revised (LSI-R; Andrews & Bonta, 1995) with respect to both general and violent recidivism. The investigators observed a small difference in favor of the LSI-R for strength of association with violent recidivism (effect sizes of .26 for the LSI-R and .21 for the PCL-R). The PCL-R is commonly used as a risk assessment standard against which other tools are compared. The authors suggested that this usage might be inappropriate in light of the slightly better performance of the LSI-R, a standard risk-needs tool. It is also worth noting that the PCL was not developed as a risk assessment measure, but as a way of assessing a specific personality disorder—so the theoretical justification for using a broader risk-needs tool is stronger.

That notwithstanding, there have been two additional meta-analyses involving the PCL-R and its relationship to violent reoffending. Walters (2003) compared the PCL-R and the Lifestyle Criminality Screening Form (a file-only measure focusing on an individual's irresponsibility, self-indulgence, interpersonal intrusiveness, and social rule-breaking; Walters, White, & Denney, 1991) in the prediction of general and violent recidivism among offenders. Both were comparably effective in this prediction ($AUC$ values were .665 for the PCL-R and .673 for the LCSF). The second meta-analysis (Leistico, Salekin, DeCoster, & Rogers, 2008) focused on the relationship between the PCL measures and a variety of forms of antisocial conduct, including criminal recidivism. They cited a significant relationship between both Factor 1 and Factor 2 scores on the PCL and recidivism risk. Factor 2 effect sizes were significantly larger than those for Factor 1. Effect sizes differed according to participant characteristics such as gender, race, and setting (correctional vs. hospital facility). This is consistent with the observation that the PCL and PCL-R are stronger predictors of reoffending in the community than of antisocial conduct in a structured setting such as a prison or a secure hospital.

## MACARTHUR RISK ASSESSMENT STUDY

These meta-analyses offer strong evidence for the potential effectiveness of actuarial prediction of violent behavior, including criminal recidivism. Moving from meta-analyses to a large-scale, multisite single study, the MacArthur Risk Assessment Study (Monahan et al., 2001; Steadman et al., 1998) is undoubtedly the largest and best-designed study of violent behavior in the community by those discharged from inpatient mental health treatment facilities. A total of 1,136 male and female patients with mental disorders between the ages of 18 and 40 were monitored for violence toward others every 10 weeks during the first year following discharge from psychiatric hospitalization, and these results were compared with violence toward others by a comparison group ($N = 519$) randomly sampled from the same census tracts as the discharged patient group. Outcome behavior was divided into two levels of severity: serious acts of violence (battery resulting in physical injury, sexual assaults, and threats with a weapon in the hand) and other aggressive acts (battery that did not result in a physical injury). Information sources included self-report (every 10 weeks), collateral report (every 10 weeks), and agency records (arrest, hospitalization).

This study yielded several important findings. First, self-report and collateral report greatly increased the sensitivity for detecting the occurrence of violence and other aggressive acts beyond the frequency reflected in official records (raising this frequency from 4.5% to 27.5% for violence and from 8.8% to 56.1% for other aggressive acts during the outcome period). Second, the presence of substance abuse increased the frequency of both serious violence and other aggressive acts. Patient participants without substance abuse did not differ from the community control group without substance abuse in the frequency of either violence or other aggressive acts, but these patient participants had symptoms of substance abuse more often than did the community controls. Third, the patient group showed a greater risk of violence and other aggressive acts than did the community controls when both experienced symptoms of substance abuse, particularly during the period immediately following hospital discharge.

The impact of "neighborhood" on violence risk in those with mental disorders was assessed in more detail through further analysis of the neighborhood variable in the Pittsburgh MacArthur site. Concentrated poverty, with associated high unemployment, racial segregation, rapid population turnover, low income levels, single-parent families with children, and limited economic opportunities, all contributed to increased violence risk beyond the effects of individual characteristics. These findings underscore the importance of considering the neighborhood context in the assessment and management of violence risk among discharged psychiatric patients in the community (Silver, Mulvey, & Monahan, 1999).

The original MacArthur data were validated using another data set (Monahan, Steadman, Robbins, et al., 2005) in the development of an actuarial tool for violence risk assessment of mentally disordered individuals in the community. This measure, the Classification of Violence Risk (COVR; Monahan, Steadman, Appelbaum, et al., 2005), is demonstrably effective in predicting serious acts of violence in the community committed by such individuals. As would be expected, there was shrinkage in the accuracy rates from the derivation to the cross-validation sample (the $AUC = .88$ dropping to an $AUC = .63–.70$, depending on the definition and measurement of outcomes). This measure, while applicable to individuals outside the criminal justice system, has not yet been researched sufficiently with individuals in the criminal justice system to determine whether it will work with them as well.

## DEBATE OVER THE USE OF ACTUARIAL MEASURES

There has been recent debate concerning actuarial measures and their application to individual cases. Hart, Michie, and Cooke (2007) suggested that wide 95% confidence intervals, which can result in overlapping categories of risk classification, limit the accuracy of actuarial prediction in a single case. Several aspects of this argument have been strongly disputed, particularly the application of Wilson's formula (1927) to a single case (see, e.g., Harris & Rice, 2007; Mossman, 2007). This formula allows the calculation of confidence intervals as a function of the number of cases, but there is disagreement about whether it is meaningful in the individual case (where $N = 1$ is inserted into the formula). Actuarial tools should be derived and validated on large samples, both to ensure that confidence intervals are narrow and the risk categories do not overlap, and to enhance generalizability. However, the suggestion that actuarial tools are not useful when applied to individual cases because confidence intervals are so wide remains open to debate. This is discussed in more detail elsewhere (see Heilbrun, Douglas, & Yasuhara, in press).

There has also been some debate over the years about the circumstances (if any) in which it is appropriate for the evaluator to adjust the weights of actuarial predictors, or to override the conclusion of the actuarial measure. A recent study (Gore, 2008) compared the accuracy of conclusions under two conditions: cases in which the conclusion of an actuarial tool (the Minnesota Sex Offender Screening Tool-Revised; Epperson et al., 2003) had been accepted, versus cases in which this conclusion had been "overridden" by clinical judgment. The investigator's conclusion was that such clinical adjustment did not make a statistically significant difference—it did not increase accuracy, but neither did it lower it. The process of weighting actuarial predictors was addressed in another study (Grann & Langstrom, 2007). Using 10 risk factors from the HCR-20, they considered the accuracy associated with four different weighting approaches (Nuffield's method, bivariate logistic regression, multivariate logistic regression, and an artificial neural network procedure). Weighting techniques of any of these four kinds did not increase accuracy over the unweighted approach, with increased weighting complexity associated with greater shrinkage of predictive accuracy on cross-validation. This may underscore the potential limits on predictive accuracy that can be attained using multiple predictors and complex weighting (Dawes, 1979; McGrath, 2008).

In an empirical study relevant to this point, Kroner, Mills, and Reddon (2005) compared the predictive accuracy of the PCL-R, LSI-R, and VRAG (three widely accepted actuarial tools), another approach that used generally recognized risk factors for recidivism, and four additional instruments that were constructed by dropping the risk factors contained in the first four into a "coffee can." These risk factors were then randomly extracted to create the additional four instruments for comparison purposes. None of the first four tools was more accurate in predicting postrelease failure than the four instruments using randomly selected risk factors from among the entire pool. The researchers suggested that these results reflected the limits of the purely actuarial approach and pointed to the need for developing a better and more comprehensive theory of violence and risk assessment in criminal justice and mental health. This remains to be tested, if such theory is forthcoming. However, these results (along with those from the previous several studies) may also point to a "ceiling effect" for predictive accuracy on violence using any approach (see Heilbrun, Yasuhara, & Shah (in press) for a fuller discussion).

## Structured Professional Judgment

SPJ tools use the consideration of specified risk factors and protective factors to yield a final judgment (typically low, moderate, or high risk) that is not quantified. However, the elements of SPJ tools can be quantified for research purposes. This is essential to demonstrate that these elements are related to outcome as they are intended. But it is also important to test SPJ tools in the way it is recommended they be used. The SPJ approach makes the assumption of a positive relationship between the number of risk factors present and the level of risk (Douglas & Kropp, 2002). This assumption, and the validity of SPJ tools, can be tested by research on the relationship between final risk judgments and outcomes. This kind of research is described in this section. In order to discuss the predictive value of elements in SPJ tools, the subsequent section will describe research that has used these elements in an actuarial fashion—and compare the resulting predictions to those yielded by existing actuarial tools.

Two recent chapters (Heilbrun, Douglas, & Yasuhara, in press; Heilbrun, Yasuhara & Shah, in press) have described 12 published studies and 1 dissertation (McGowan, 2007) that investigate the link between final SPJ risk judgments and violence. Eleven of these studies suggested that SPJ judgments are significantly predictive of violent recidivism (Catchpole & Gretton, 2003; de Vogel & de Ruiter, 2005, 2006; de Vogel et al., 2004; Douglas, Ogloff, & Hart, 2003; Douglas, Yeomans, & Boer, 2005; Enebrink et al., 2006; Kropp & Hart, 2000; McGowan, 2007; Meyers & Schmidt, 2008; Welsh, Schmidt, McKinnon, Chattha, & Meyers, 2008). Two of the 13 studies (Sjösted & Långström, 2002; Viljoen et al., 2008), in contrast, did not support a significant relationship between SPJ judgments and target outcomes. Five studies addressed the additional question of whether the SPJ "final judgment" adds incremental predictive validity to the actuarial combination of the tool elements. Incremental validity was observed in all five of these studies (de Vogel et al., 2006; Douglas et al., 2003, 2005; Enebrink et al., 2006; Kropp & Hart, 2000).

The research base for SPJ approaches to risk assessment is more limited than that of actuarial approaches. This is due to the much more recent development of SPJ; such tools and associated research began appearing in the 1990s. An overview of the existing studies on SPJ does suggest that it is an efficacious approach to risk assessment, consistent with empirically supported best practice. But there is still a question of how it might compare generally with actuarial approaches. They are not fully distinct approaches—they are similar in their approaches to data selection (using specified elements with an empirical relationship to the target outcome) and data coding (operationalizing the elements on the tool so they can be coded reliably). But they differ in data combination. Actuarial measures combine data using a heuristic developed and validated on specific data sets, and then cross-validated on separate data sets. SPJ "structures" the final conclusion regarding risk by requiring the evaluator to consider the specified elements included in the measure. So it is reasonable to assume that observed differences between these approaches are attributable to the different ways in which they combine data.

**INFO**

Actuarial and SPJ approaches are similar in data selection and data coding, but differ in data combination.

## Actuarial Versus Structured Professional Judgment Approaches

Several studies have compared SPJ measures—combining their elements in actuarial fashion to yield a final score related to risk—with actuarial tools that are also used in this way. One study (Douglas et al., 2005) compared the HCR-20 (an SPJ measure; Webster et al., 1997), used in this fashion, with the Violence Risk Appraisal Guide (VRAG; Harris et al., 1993), PCL-R (Hare, 1991), and the Psychopathy Checklist-Screening Version (PCL-SV; Hart, Cox, & Hare, 1995) (actuarial tools). Large effects were observed for HCR-20 structured risk judgments, VRAG total scores, and behavioral scales of psychopathy measures. These findings supported several aspects of the actuarial approach to risk assessment, but also provided support for the final risk judgment of the HCR-20 (not a result of actuarial data combination). Similar results were observed in a study in Germany comparing the HCR-20, PCL-R, and LSI-R (Dahle, 2006). There were only small and statistically nonsignificant differences in predictive accuracy among these three measures, with both VRAG total score and HCR-20 final risk judgment significant when the regression was conducted using direct entry. Stepwise entry, in which the software identifies the strongest predictor (rather than the investigator indicating which variable should be entered first), yielded significance for the HCR-20 overall risk judgment.

One further study did yield a conclusion more favorable to an SPJ measure (the SVR-20; Boer, Hart, Kropp, & Webster, 1997) than an actuarial measure (the Static-99; Hanson & Thornton, 1999) for assessing sexual reoffense risk. Using file information to complete the SVR-20 and the Static-99 on hospitalized sexual offenders ($N = 122$) in the Netherlands subsequently released to the community and tracked over a mean outcome period of about 12 years, they measured the predictive validity of both measures using ROC analysis. Levels of predictive validity were good for all measures, but significantly better for SVR-20 total score ($AUC = .80$) and final risk judgment ($AUC = .83$) than for Static-99 total score ($AUC = .71$).

A fourth study (Catchpole & Gretton, 2003) compared two actuarial approaches and an SPJ approach with adolescents ($N = 133$) referred by juvenile judges. The Youth Level of Service/Case

Management Inventory (YLS/CMI; Hoge & Andrews, 2002) and the Psychopathy Checklist: Youth Version (PCL:YV; Forth, Kosson, & Hare, 2003), as well as the Structured Assessment of Violence Risk in Youth (SAVRY; Borum, Bartel, & Forth, 2005), were compared. The average follow-up period was 35.8 months (outcome periods ranged from 7 to 61 months). The SPJ tool (the SAVRY) was the most accurate, according to the ROC analyses conducted with all three tools (SAVRY $AUC = .81$, PCL:SV $AUC = .73$, and YLS/CMI $AUC = .64$).

It is clear that the enhanced structure associated with either actuarial or SPJ approaches increases assessment accuracy (Monahan, 2008). However, one implication of the Kroner et al. (2005) study, in which investigators found that the random combination of established risk factors was as accurate as their combination in an established tool, is that we may be reaching a ceiling in predictive accuracy. Additional research (and perhaps more sophisticated theory regarding violent behavior) will help us determine whether this ceiling effect is stable, or whether predictive accuracy can be increased further.

This limited number of studies must be increased to strengthen our confidence about any conclusions involving a comparison between actuarial and SJP measures. In addition, we must consider that there is probably variability between the quality of different actuarial measures, and between various SJP measures. As a result, it is not straightforward to conclude that the comparison between an actuarial tool and an SJP measure has strong implications for the overall method rather than the specific tool. With that said, however, we can conclude that existing evidence suggests that these two approaches are empirically supported at comparable levels. Two studies even suggested some advantage in predictive accuracy to the SJP approach. Until further research is available to refine this conclusion, it would appear that the use of either an actuarial or SPJ specialized risk assessment tool is consistent with best practice in FMHA risk assessment from the standpoint of empirical support.

**INFO**

Actuarial and SPJ approaches to risk assessment are empirically supported at comparable levels.

## Anamnestic Approaches

The anamnestic approach is designed to obtain a detailed picture of an individual's functioning. Used in the context of risk assessment, it seeks to identify dynamic risk factors, particularly those that are targets for intervention and are also useful for risk

management, by using the evaluee's history of violence. It is not well suited to making predictions, nor does it yield much useful information if the evaluee has little history of violence. When there is such a history, however, it can potentially provide information that is not readily available from other measures or sources (Dvoskin & Heilbrun, 2001). It offers a targeted, analytic procedure for "individualizing" the assessment of risk. In addition, it provides a commonsense basis for obtaining information that is relevant to future violence. Is there a more potent source of information that is as readily appreciated by legal decision makers than a detailed account of the evaluee's prior violence? Is there a more face-valid way of gauging risk factors applicable to that individual? Finally, it can identify the occasional exceptional case when using the evaluee's history would be misleading, given a substantial change in personal or situational influences.

## Specialized Risk Assessment Tools

This section will discuss four specialized risk assessment tools in this section: the VRAG (Harris et al., 1993), the COVR (Monahan Steadman, Appelbaum et al., 2005), the LS/CMI (Andrews et al., 2004), and the HCR-20 (Webster et al., 1997). These were selected for several reasons. First, they are among the best specialized measures of risk that are available, with strong conceptual and empirical support. Second, they represent measures that are prediction oriented and actuarial (the VRAG and COVR), risk needs and actuarial (the LS/CMI), and risk needs and SPJ (the HCR-20). In this respect, they are representative of the kinds of measures that have helped strengthening the empirical foundations of FMHA risk assessment with adults. Reviewing all (or even most) available tools is beyond the scope of this book, but the present review of empirical strength combined with a comparison of these tools on a number of additional dimensions (see Table 5.1) can provide a model for reviewing other risk assessment measures.

## Violence Risk Appraisal Guide

The VRAG is a 12-item actuarial guide that was developed and supported through extensive research conducted by Canadian investigators. This program of research is summarized in two books (Quinsey, Harris, Rice, & Cormier, 1998, 2006). In several respects, it represents an exemplary approach to the development and validation of a specialized measure: (1) a fairly large data set (685 men, of whom 618 had the opportunity to recidivate; see Rice, Harris, & Cormier, 1992; Rice, Harris, Lang, & Bell, 1990), (2) programmatic research spanning two decades, (3) a clear purpose (the identification of relative and quantitative levels of risk through actuarial assessment), and (4) clearly operationalized outcome measures (rearrest for a violent offense; institutional violence; adaptations for specific violence such as sexual offending and fire-setting).

The empirical support for the VRAG is extensive. Independent coding of variables by trained raters yielded a correlation of .90, suggesting high reliability of coding at the total score level (Harris et al., 1993), a finding that has been replicated several times (Harris, Rice, & Cormier, 2002; Harris, Rice, & Quinsey, 2003). VRAG predictive accuracy does not depend on the base rate of violence, according to ROC analysis (Rice & Harris, 1995). The ROC $AUC$ values for violent offenders and a higher-risk subpopulation of sexual offenders, over a 10-year outcome period, were in the .73–.77 range (Quinsey et al., 2006). VRAG scores predicted

violent recidivism well ($AUC = .80$) in a cohort of 347 male forensic patients who were scored on the VRAG prior to release (Harris
et al., 2002). A modified (10-item) version of the VRAG predicted
post-discharge serious acts of violence in the MacArthur sample
(see COVR discussion, following) at 20- and 50-week follow-up
($AUC = .72$). Indeed, the predictive accuracy of the VRAG has
ranged from .60 to .85 ($AUC$ values) over a variety of antisocial
outcomes among forensic psychiatric patients, including sexual
offending, fire-setting, and institutional violence (Quinsey et al.,
2006). There is strong support, therefore, for the conclusion that
the VRAG is a valid tool for the prediction of criminal violence (and
specific other antisocial outcomes).

There is one respect in which the VRAG is potentially problematic. It has nine categories, each associated with a mean level of risk
specified for each category. These categories overlap somewhat
within 95% confidence intervals. The authors note that "overlap
among categories and confidence intervals was not great . . . reliability was sufficiently high that we were confident that an individual's actual risk did not differ by much more than one category
from his obtained score" (Quinsey et al., 2006, p. 165). For maximal value in risk communication, it would be preferably to have
categories that do not overlap at all within 95% confidence intervals. The evaluator must consider this caveat in using VRAG results
to describe a certain level of risk. A related point calls for clarity
rather than criticism. The VRAG outcome period with the
expanded database is 10 years. This is an appropriate outcome
period for some FMHA risk assessment questions, but overly long
for others. The evaluator should be guided by the outcome period
most appropriate to the legal question being evaluating in deciding
whether the VRAG is indicated—although there is some evidence
(see Quinsey et al., 2006) that the VRAG is reasonably accurate in
predicting shorter-term outcomes as well.

## Classification of Violence Risk

The COVR (Monahan Steadman, Appelbaum, et al., 2005) is the
tool that was developed specifically from the MacArthur Risk
Assessment study (described earlier in this chapter) followed by an

independent cross-validation. Both the original study (Monahan et al., 2001; Steadman et al., 1998) and the cross-validation study (Monahan, Steadman, Robbins, et al., 2005) were conducted with individuals in the community who had been hospitalized for psychiatric reasons and subsequently returned to the community. The original MacArthur risk assessment study was the single largest and best-designed investigation ever conducted on community violence among individuals with mental disorder, many of them with severe mental illness. It consists of a series of questions and probes (up to 27, depending on how many initial questions are answered "yes") that are administered by entering the responses into a computer program. Responses are scored using decision tree analysis, yielding one of five categories of risk of a serious act of violence over the next several months: very low risk (1%, 95% confidence interval 0–2%), low risk (8%, 95% confidence interval 5–11%), average risk (26%, 95% confidence interval 20–32%), high risk (56%, 95% confidence interval 46–65%), and very high risk (76%, 95% confidence interval 65–86%). These categories do not overlap, within 95% confidence intervals. This measure shares some of the developmental strengths of the VRAG. It was developed from a large data set and cross-validated independently. The original study took over 5 years to complete. The COVR is clearly identified as a predictive tool, and the outcome measure (serious acts of violence) is a carefully defined and measured behavioral variable.

The empirical foundation for the COVR is extremely strong. It would be unusual to say that about a measure that was derived from a single study and cross-validated through another single study. However, these were two of the methodologically strongest and most rigorous studies imaginable. The original study (Steadman et al., 1998) included three sites: Kansas City, Worcester, and Pittsburgh. The mental health facilities and participant demographics differed across sites, enhancing the external validity. The addition of Philadelphia as an additional site (as well as using Worcester again) in the cross-validation study (Monahan, Steadman, Robbins, et al., 2005) added to the geographic and facility diversity used in the development of this tool. The accuracy of the tool's prediction was very strong for the derivation sample ($AUC$ = .88) and somewhat lower for the cross-validation sample ($AUC$ = .63–.70, depending on the definition and measurement of outcomes). Two additional strengths of the COVR are noteworthy. First, the outcome variable was operationalized using self-report, collateral report, and official records. All the other specialized measures reviewed in this chapter, and most others in existence, use some version of official records—which the researchers found to be far less sensitive than either self- or collateral report. It is apparent, therefore, that the measurement of outcome is more accurate than it would have been using official records alone. Second, the development and analytic strategy was particularly sophisticated. It included eight steps: identifying gaps in methodology, selecting promising risk factors, using tree-based methods, creating different cutoff scores for high and low risk, repeating the classification tree, combining multiple risk estimates, developing the COVR software, and prospectively validating the software. This process might fairly be described as painstakingly careful and methodologically sophisticated.

The COVR has several limitations. As a prediction-oriented tool, it was not designed to yield information about risk reduction, so individuals involved in the treatment of hospitalized individuals would seek this information separately. (Since the COVR is quite efficient to administer and score, taking an average of 10 minutes by a trained interviewer who is not necessarily a clinician, it still remains an effective investment of time.) It is also somewhat limited by the very complex nature of the analytic strategy. When the COVR is used in FMHA risk assessment (perhaps as part of civil commitment proceedings), the explanation for how the information was analyzed by the software would not be easily understood by someone not trained in statistical analysis. Accordingly, evaluators must develop a "lay version" of decision tree analysis that includes an explanation of how the decision was reached and why it could not be calculated by hand or checked with paper and pencil.

## Level of Service/Case Management Inventory

The LS/CMI (Andrews et al., 2004) is the third iteration in the series of Level of Service Inventories. It is a risk-needs tool composed of 43 items in the following areas: criminal history, education/ employment, family/marital, leisure/recreation, companions, alcohol/drug problem, procriminal attitude/orientation, and antisocial pattern. It also has sections including specific risk/need factors (personal problems with criminogenic potential, history of perpetration), prison experience (for those with an incarceration history, including past incarceration and present incarceration), barriers to release, social/health/mental health, and special responsivity issues. It combines the scores from items on criminal history in Section 1 into a single score that yields one of five risk levels: very low (0–4), low (5–10), medium (11–19), high (20–29), and very high (30+). Recidivism is defined as a new incarceration within 1 year after release from prison. Recidivism rates (but no confidence intervals) are provided for each of these levels; the conclusion (risk level and implications) is reached using an actuarial approach by combining the risk factors in an unweighted fashion. Like the VRAG and the COVR, the LS/CMI and its two previous iterations were developed and validated using large data sets. The supporting research has been ongoing for nearly two decades. It has been conceptualized and used as a risk-needs tool from its inception, using an outcome (reincarceration within 1 year) that is narrower and hence less frequent than the violent rearrest used by the VRAG, and different from the "serious acts of violence" criterion used by the COVR.

The normative groups for the earlier version (the LSI-R; Andrews & Bonta, 1995) included both males and females. A total of 956 males from the Ottawa-Carleton Detention Centre, Hamilton-Wentworth Detention Centre, and Toronto Jail were considered; the mean age was 26.9, mean sentence length 325.6 days, and mean number of convictions 3.7. Offenses included 26.4% crimes against persons, 50.9% crimes against property, 9.8% drug offenses, 8.2% alcohol/traffic offenses, and the remainder were miscellaneous. The female sample was composed of 1,414 females from a medium-security institution for adult women operated by Ontario Ministry of Correctional Services. The mean age of individuals in this sample was 30.2, and the mean sentence 322 days. Reliability was generally good; there was high agreement ($r = .80–.94$) between trained raters, who included, at times, correctional officers.

Test–retest reliability decreased some over time, as would be expected with change in risk factors (Andrews & Bonta, 1995). Using meta-analysis, Gendreau et al. (2002) compared the predictive performance of the PCL-R (Hare, 1991) with that of the LSI-R with respect to both general and violent recidivism. A small difference was seen in favor of the LSI-R for strength of association with violent recidivism (effect sizes of .26 for the LSI-R and .21 for the PCL-R), which appeared unlikely to be attributable to chance. Such meta-analytic findings are consistent with both the strength of the LSI-R as a predictive tool, and its slightly better performance in this respect than that of the PCL-R—which has often been treated as a benchmark of predictive accuracy against which other measures are compared.

The LS/CMI is an updated version of the previous Level of Service Inventories, so it does not need full and independent validation; the evidence suggests that it performs comparably to the prior versions. There are two particular limitations to this tool. It is applicable to a general offender population, and hence may provide less specific intervention guidance than a tool developed more specifically for a population of mentally disordered offenders (such as the HCR-20, described next). Given that it uses reincarceration as the outcome, it may be less sensitive to reoffending resulting in arrest but not conviction, or conviction but not reincarceration. It may, in other words, underestimate risk for antisocial behavior that does not result in the individual's reincarceration within 1 year. The second limitation involves the apparent absence of confidence intervals surrounding the cited rates of recidivism for the different categories of risk, making it difficult to determine whether the categories overlap.

## HCR-20

The HCR-20 (Historic, Clinical, Risk Management; Webster et al., 1997) is a risk-needs tool that uses SPJ in having the evaluator describe a final risk rating after reviewing all 20 items in these three areas. They include Historic items (previous violence, young age at first violent incident, relationship instability, employment problems, substance use problems, major mental illness, psychopathy, early maladjustment, personality disorder, and prior supervision failure), Clinical items (lack of insight, negative attitudes, active symptoms of major mental illness, impulsivity, and unresponsiveness to treatment), and Risk Management items (lack of feasibility in plans, exposure to destabilizers, lack of personal support, noncompliance with remediation attempts, and stress). Like the other tools reviewed in this section, the HCR-20 has been empirically studied from initial validation research to additional research over the last decade in North America and Europe. It has been clearly conceptualized as a risk-needs tool, using SPJ in rendering a final risk estimate. This necessarily yields two strategies in validation research: studying the "H" section factors in actuarial fashion to determine their relationship to subsequent violence, and studying the extent to which individuals identified with final risk judgment at higher risk are more likely to engage in violence than those identified with such judgments at lower risk. Both strategies have been used to study this tool.

Initial validation research using the HCR-20 involved reviewing the files of 193 civilly committed patients in Canada which were coded retrospectively using the HCR-20 and the PCL-SV. Follow-up data were obtained in the community over an average of 626 days using official records (provincial correctional files, which include court and correctional contacts, and hospital readmission records as well as admission to any of 16 general hospitals throughout province, and coroner's death records). Persons scoring above the HCR-20 median (19, of a possible total of 40) were 6–13 times more likely to be violent during outcome period. The HCR-20 added incremental validity to PCL-SV (Douglas, Ogloff, Nicholls, & Grant, 1999). In addition, the files of 75 male, Canadian, federally sentenced maximum security inmates were coded using the HCR-20, PCL-R, and VRAG. The HCR-20 was as strongly related to past violence as either PCL-R or VRAG. Scores above the median (19) of the HCR-20 increased the odds of past violent and antisocial behavior by an average of 4 times (Douglas & Webster, 1999). Subsequently, Douglas and colleagues (2005) compared the respective predictive validities of the HCR-20 and several other tools, including the VRAG, PCL-R, and PCL:SV, among others. Large effect sizes for violent recidivism with obtained for HCR-20 structured risk judgments, VRAG scores, and behavioral scales of psychopathy measures. Similar results supporting the relationship between SPJ final risk judgments and violent outcomes have been obtained by others as well (Dahle, 2006; de Vogel & de Ruiter, 2005, 2006; Douglas et al., 2005). Thus, there appears to be strong support for the relationship between the HCR-20 and violence, whether the investigation involves using the "H" section score as a quantitative predictor or using final risk judgment as the basis for prediction. In addition, the focus on dynamic risk factors (Douglas & Skeem, 2005) is consistent with the measurement of changing risk levels, and with recent research approaching such change over very short durations (Skeem et al., 2006).

There are limitations to the HCR-20 as well. As an SPJ tool, it has a strong demonstrated relationship to violence as an outcome. However, the tool does not allow the evaluator to anchor the judgment of risk level within a quantitative range. The evaluator may therefore conclude that an individual is at high risk for future violence based on a review of the entire HCR-20 results, but cannot answer the question "how high is high?" or compare well across populations. The second limitation involved the extent to which HCR-20 results address specific implications for risk reduction treatment. The original tool provided clinical and risk management items that could be interpreted fairly broadly but had fewer specific implications for intervention. This limitation has largely been addressed through the publication of the *HCR-20 Violence Risk Management Companion Guide* (Douglas, Webster, Hart, Eaves, & Ogloff, 2001), however.

# Scientifically Supported, Unsupported, and Controversial Uses of Risk Assessment

In a recent chapter, Heilbrun, Douglas, Yasuhara et al. (in press) discussed existing scientific evidence and controversies in risk assessment. We drew some conclusions about practices in risk assessment that are consistent with scientific evidence, unsupported by scientific evidence, and controversial or untested (needing more evidence, in effect). These will be discussed to provide a capstone for the material described earlier in this chapter.

## Scientifically Supported Uses

- *Conclusions that persons scoring higher on validated actuarial risk assessment instruments or rated as higher risk on validated SPJ instruments are at greater risk for violence than those scoring lower on these instruments.* There is a great deal of evidence that validated risk assessment tools provide a way of effectively distinguishing those at different levels of risk for violence, violent offending, and certain other antisocial outcomes.

- *Actuarial prediction strategies for group-based predictions, with large derivation and validation samples, using mean probability and including margin of error.* One of the most effective ways in which actuarial measures can be applied is in distinguishing one group from another in terms of relative risk. A hospital or correctional facility might use a tool such as the VRAG to distinguish those at higher risk for institutional misconduct from those at lower risk; particularly if the overlapping categories problem could be managed (e.g., through using the highest three categories and the lowest three categories only, and combining them into "low-risk" and "high-risk" groups), this would be a powerful and accurate tool in making an informed decision on this point.

- *Use of extreme risk categories as more informative and less subject to limits of overlapping confidence intervals.* When categories do not overlap, the evaluator can be more confident that a score within one category is not likely (within the limits of 95% confidence) to connote membership in a different category. Using extreme risk categories solves that problem, and may provide information that is more useful for legal decision making than is offered by information about intermediate levels of risk.

- *Indication that application of group-based data to an individual case or small number of cases will result in wider confidence intervals than application to a large number of cases.* It seems clear that large samples in the derivation and validation of actuarial tools not only enhance generalizability, but they also shrink the size of the confidence intervals associated with particular categories. Narrower confidence intervals translate into greater confidence that the mean is an accurate representation of that category.

## Scientifically Unsupported Uses

- *Actuarial prediction strategies without large derivation and validation samples.* The actuarial development and validation of a risk assessment tool is a rigorous process, requiring large samples and replication. The use of smaller samples and the failure to include independent validation is likely to yield a measure that is overly influenced by error variance.

- *Actuarial prediction strategies applied to populations that are not part of the derivation and validation samples.* There must be empirical evidence that any strategy that is part of a specialized risk assessment measure is applicable to a given population before that measure can be fairly applied in practice. Actuarial strategies are noted here particularly because they provide specific, quantitative estimates of risk; such specificity can be checked empirically for accuracy. But the larger point would apply to any specialized tool using either an actuarial or SPJ approach. For example, a measure developed with a population of mentally disordered offenders should not be applied to those undergoing civil commitment without empirical evidence that the measure is applicable.

- *Conclusions that a given "individual" has an X probability of violence in the future, without the context of confidence intervals and the caution about less certainty in the individual case.* If an individual receives a score that places him in a given risk category, it is appropriate to know whether that category overlaps (within 95% confidence) with others. It is also important to be somewhat more cautious about the conclusion drawn about an individual than the conclusion that would be drawn if the measure were applied to a group.

## Scientifically Controversial and/or Largely Untested Uses

- *Actuarial prediction strategies with large derivation and validation samples using mean probability but not citing margin of error and its increased uncertainty when applied to single cases.* This is another way of emphasizing the immediately previous point. Even actuarial measures that are developed with large samples should use risk communication language incorporating confidence intervals. "Uncertainty about the individual" can be handled through strategies "individualizing" the assessment, discussed elsewhere in this book.

- *The assumption that there are reliable, known probability estimates that are robust across samples, even at the group level.* This will be one of the most interesting questions addressed through research in the next 10 years. It may be that good specialized risk assessment tools, such as those described in this chapter, tap a broad, robust set of factors that *do* generalize across populations, outcomes, and settings. At present, however, it is best to emphasize the application of specialized measures only to the populations on which and outcomes for which they were developed, unless they are appropriately validated for different ones.

# Conclusion

This chapter reviewed the evidence on actuarial and SPJ approaches to risk assessment, and tools that are primarily predictive versus those that assess both risk and needs. Fairly limited evidence is available comparing the accuracy of predictions made using actuarial and SPJ approaches, but existing evidence suggests that the two are comparable. Additional and ongoing research will help determine whether this conclusion is accurate. The empirical foundations and limits of four specialized risk assessment tools were described; additional discussion of the various aspects of these tools is offered in Chapter 5. Finally, the conclusions concerning scientifically supported, unsupported, and controversial assumptions in risk assessment may provide some guidance for the use of science in considering best practice in FMHA risk assessment.

# APPLICATION

# Preparation
# for the Evaluation | **4**

.

The next step in conducting FMHA risk assessment involves planning, and this chapter will discuss several aspects of such planning. First, it will describe the important step of specifying the referral questions related to violence risk. Because of the range of questions encompassed by the different legal questions that include risk assessment, this is a particularly important start. It entails outlining the indicated aspects of risk assessment through legal sources and model applications, and considering the variables of *population* and *parameters*. Part of this discussion will also focus on the sources of information that are useful in conducting FMHA risk assessment.

The next aspect of planning concerns the process of working with attorneys in such evaluations. There is considerable overlap between the information that is relevant to this topic, and the broader question of how the forensic clinician works with attorneys in other kinds of FMHA. Indeed, such overlap is an issue with the remaining topics in this chapter as well. There is no need to repeat what has been written elsewhere in detail (see, e.g., Heilbrun, Grisso, & Goldstein, 2008; Melton, Petrila, Poythress, & Slobogin, 2007) on these topics, although the importance of clarifying one's role with the attorney and retaining that role throughout the evaluation, and obtaining appropriate authorization, deserve mention. The focus will be on how they apply to forensic evaluations of risk assessment. There are several particular points that need to be addressed in regards to working with attorneys in the risk assessment context, including questions involving observation and participation; these will be discussed accordingly.

Evaluation logistics will be discussed subsequently. In some respects, this discussion will preview a more detailed treatment of the safety considerations involved in evaluating individuals who are potentially violent (provided in Chapter 5). An account of planning for third party information, particularly collateral interviews, will follow. The final section of this chapter will discuss important ethical issues pertaining to consent or notification of purpose that arise in working with both evaluees and collateral interviewees.

## Identifying Specific Questions Within the Referral: Determining the Scope and Focus of the Evaluation

### Risk of What?

An initial important question in FMHA risk assessment is "risk of what?" There is a variety of outcomes that may be addressed in different kinds of risk assessment, ranging from any kind of criminal offending to more specific kinds of offenses (e.g., sexual offenses) to threats of harm as well as actual violence toward others (in the course of civil commitment, for example). So it is very important to consider the nature and scope of the acts that are contemplated in the specific risk assessment being conducted. There are two particular reasons for this. First it is important that any FMHA consider the components of the legal question; with risk assessment, this means that the evaluator should attempt to appraise the risk of conduct that is most consistent with the outcomes defined by the law in this kind of case. The second reason involves the choice of a specialized risk assessment tool. Such tools add substantially to the empirically supported foundations of risk assessment, and it is consistent with best practice to use a specialized tool when appropriate. But the tool must have been developed using outcomes that are reasonably similar to the kind of conduct considered by the law if it is to have direct applicability in the assessment. Of course, the evaluator can always use a tool that has been validated using a more limited outcome than the law considers relevant, and this discrepancy can be addressed at the interpretation, reasoning, and communication stages. However, it is difficult or impossible to use a tool validated on a range of behavior that is broader than that contemplated by the legal question and to use the results meaningfully.

Two examples will illustrate this point. First, a forensic clinician who is evaluating an individual found Not Guilty by Reason of Insanity and committed for involuntary hospitalization may observe that the criteria for continuing such hospitalization are broad. "Danger to self or others," the standard in many U.S. jurisdictions, may be interpreted broadly to include any criminal offending, even minor acts of theft (see *Jones v. United States*, 1983). Using a specialized tool such as the VRAG (Harris, Rice, & Quinsey, 1993) would help the evaluator calculate the risk of future acts of violence leading to hospitalization or arrests for violent offenses. However, since "danger to others" covers a domain of behavior broader than this outcome, the evaluator would need to compensate for this limitation by providing additional information about the individual's risk for other acts that are illegal. By contrast, a forensic clinician evaluating an individual for classification as a Sexually Violent Predator (see Witt & Conroy, 2008) may focus primarily or exclusively on the risk of future sexual offending. Using a tool normed on outcomes of general offending and violent offending, such as the LS/CMI (Andrews, Bonta, & Wormith, 2004), would possibly provide an unwarranted estimate of risk by focusing too broadly. The latter problem, it seems, would be virtually impossible to disentangle at the interpretation, reasoning, or communication stages of FMHA risk assessment.

## What Kind of Opinion on Risk Is Needed?

The next important question in the focus planning involves whether it is only a prediction or risk classification that is needed, or whether the legal question is usefully informed by opinions regarding both risk and needs. The substantial literature on corrections rehabilitation incorporating risk, needs, and responsivity (Andrews & Bonta, 2006) and the related distinction between prediction and management in risk assessment (Heilbrun, 1997) reflect the availability of specialized tools that are exclusively predictive (e.g., the VRAG) or

risk needs (e.g., the LS/CMI). But the prediction versus management distinction may also be seen in the context of existing legal questions. Depending on the nature of the legal question being addressed in the FMHA risk assessment, the opinion that is needed may be for risk level—or both risk and associated needs.

## To What Population Does the Individual Belong?

The contributions of legal parameters and specialized tool availability also apply when specifying the next question: the population to which the individual being evaluated belongs. In addition, population is important because its specification links the risk assessment with a broader empirical literature on individuals within that population. There are several important parameters in describing population.

### LEGAL STATUS

This involves the question of whether the individual is under civil, criminal, or family court jurisdiction, with further specification in family court of delinquent versus dependent proceedings.

### AGE

Adults and adolescents make up the great majority of individuals appraised for their risk toward others using FMHA risk assessment. Preadolescents constitute a third distinct category into which an individual can be placed.

### GENDER

Some of the scientific evidence discussed earlier in this book suggests that males and females share certain risk factors for violence. However, the research is more extensive with males, and there may be additional risk factors, or different interpretation of similar risk factors, that apply to females. For these reasons, gender is an important aspect of the population description.

## MENTAL HEALTH STATUS

One important distinction when describing population concerns whether the individual is part of a population selected (at least in part) for reasons related to mental health symptoms, particularly the presence of serious mental illness.

## LOCATION OF THE INDIVIDUAL BEING EVALUATED

This is used to distinguish broadly between populations that have been hospitalized or incarcerated (and hence are being considered for continued hospitalization or incarceration

**BEST PRACTICE**

In order to link the risk assessment with a broader empirical literature on a specific population, consider an evaluee's

● legal status,

● age,

● gender,

● mental health status,

● location.

vs. some form of release) from those being considered for initial placement, hospitalization, or incarceration. The question of where the individual will be placed during the period in which violence risk is appraised is also important. However, it is noted under the parameters of the evaluation in the next subsection.

## What Are the Relevant Parameters of the Risk Assessment?

Planning continues with the specification of the *parameters* of the FMHA risk assessment. This expands upon the "risk of what" question noted earlier. It begins with the question of what behavior is being included in the outcome definition, but continues by adding details to the specification.

### FREQUENCY

For some risk assessment, the single occurrence of a target behavior during the outcome period is sufficient to conclude that the outcome has been "positive"—that is, the predicted behavior has occurred. When the targeted outcome is less serious, however, there may be interest in predicting not only the occurrence of the target behavior, but the number of times it occurs.

### LOCATION

The question of where the appraised individual will be during the outcome period is linked to the related question of where they were placed at the time of the evaluation (see previous subsection). There can be a substantial difference between violence in the community and violence in a hospital or correctional facility in a variety of respects, including the level of monitoring and the like-lihood of detection. This question becomes more complex when the individual's current location and their location during the out-come period differ, as when an individual in prison is appraised for risk of sexual offending in the community following release.

### LIKELIHOOD

The manner in which the opinion will be communicated is another important consideration. Specialized tools may allow the results to be communicated in terms of probability ("Mr. Jones is 50% likely to commit a violent act during the next 6 months"), frequency ("Mr. Jones's score places him in a category in which 50% of the individuals are observed to commit an act of violence during the 6 months following release"), or risk category ("Mr. Jones's score places him in the high-risk category, a group in which 50% of indi-viduals—with the 95% confidence interval 48%–52%—commit a violent act during the next 6 months"). The probability approach may be the most appropriate way to convey the final opinion regarding risk when the evaluator is striving for an individualized conclusion. But whenever numbers are used, there should be a clear and justifiable basis for their inclusion.

### NATURE OF RISK AND PROTECTIVE FACTORS

One substantial advantage in using a specialized risk assessment tool involves the structure of such a tool. Important risk factors (and sometimes protective factors) are specified as a part of this tool. Hence, the evaluator does not need to select such factors from the broader literature. However, there may be applicable risk or protective factors that are not specified by a risk assessment tool. These must be identified by other means, and their impact weighed as part of the overall FMHA risk assessment.

**BEST PRACTICE**

In addition to what behavior is being included in the outcome definition, specify the following parameters:

- Frequency
- Location
- Likelihood
- Nature of risk and protective factors

## Sources of Information

**BEST PRACTICE**

Obtain both nomothetic and idiographic data for the FMHA risk assessment.

Planning to conduct a risk assessment as part of FMHA is affected by the nomothetic–idiographic distinction that is observed in forensic assessment (see Heilbrun, 2001).

*Nomothetic* data, obtained through group-referenced conventional scientific research, focus primarily on differences between groups. *Idiographic* data, obtained through sources focusing only on the individual being evaluated, typically address differences within that individual, and between that person and an abstract legal standard (e.g., a reasonable person).

Best practice in FMHA calls for obtaining both nomothetic and idiographic information. In the context of risk assessment, nomothetic data are obtained through specialized risk assessment tools and perhaps broader psychological tests. Idiographic information is drawn from multiple sources, including interviews with the individual and third parties, and relevant records. The "Collateral Information" section in this chapter describes particular sources of third party information that are most applicable to risk assessment, as well as strategies for enhancing the accuracy of third party interviews.

**4** chapter

# Working With Attorneys: Attorney Representation, Involvement, Control and Authority Pertaining to the Evaluation

The next stage in the planning process involves contact with attorneys. Most of this contact will occur with the attorney who has referred the case for evaluation. This may be the lawyer who represents the evaluee in the ongoing litigation; less often, it is the prosecutor in a criminal case seeking a rebuttal opinion in response to an initial evaluation conducted by another forensic clinician.

Any individual considered for evaluation in a forensic context should be represented by counsel (Committee on Ethical Guidelines for Forensic Psychologists, 1991). This ensures that the individual's legal rights are protected, and also facilitates logistical tasks such as obtaining records and scheduling the evaluation.

The question of whether either attorney—defense counsel and prosecutor in criminal matters, plaintiff's and defense counsel in civil litigation—can observe the risk assessment evaluation is somewhat complex. This will be discussed from the standpoint of what is reasonable and important in conducting the best possible evaluation. As in any forensic assessment, these considerations may be overridden by legal arguments culminating in a court order. Having the individual's attorney *observe* the evaluation is not a particular problem. The problems arise when that attorney moves from fully passive observer to adviser/participant, however minor the participation may seem. An attorney who advises her client against responding to questions that are part of the evaluation, or attempts to influence the nature of these responses in any way, can actually alter the course of the evaluation and affect the resulting data. This is not acceptable. If there are topics that would otherwise be investigated in the course of the evaluation, but to which the attorney objects for legal reasons, this should be addressed before the evaluation has commenced and a ruling obtained from the court. For example, many kinds of risk assessment would investigate the individual's history of criminal offending. This might include a history of acts for which the individual could have been arrested if apprehended, but was not caught. An attorney might reasonably attempt to exclude such questions. If this attempt were successful, and the judge held *a priori* that such questions could not be asked, then the evaluator should abide by this ruling and perhaps note its potential impact on his final opinions. But it would not be acceptable to have the same attorney, while observing the evaluation, instruct her client not to respond to this question. Such behavior is disruptive to the evaluation and may affect its integrity in other ways. (Among other considerations, an evaluator who knew before beginning the risk assessment that certain questions could not be asked might consider alternative ways to obtain comparable information that were legally acceptable. This cannot necessarily be done without advance notice and preparation, however.)

Thus, allowing the attorney who represents the person being evaluated to observe is not particularly problematic, as long as this is managed in a way that allows the attorney to observe (and even record) but not participate. The question of whether opposing counsel can observe is perhaps less complex. (In the author's anecdotal experience, this is also extremely rare. Having personally conducted or supervised approximately 2700 forensic evaluations in his professional career, the author can recall only a handful of instances in which opposing counsel asked to observe the evaluation.) There would need to be a compelling reason, as well as legal authority in the form of a court order, to allow observation by the opposing counsel. Such observation could be particularly problematic in risk assessment, given the sensitivity of much of the information that is sought. However, documentation of the entire evaluation will be available to both attorneys in the course of the proceedings if a report is submitted. As with other FMHA, such documentation should be careful and comprehensive (Committee on Ethical Guidelines for Forensic Psychologists, 1991).

4
chapter

## Evaluation Logistics: When, Where, Within What Period, and Under What Authorization

FMHA risk assessment is not substantially different from other kinds of FMHA with respect to logistics. Put somewhat differently, the variability in such logistics across different kinds of risk assessments is probably as great as the variability across the entire range of FMHA. So it is not useful to discuss such logistics—with one exception. The evaluation of the risk of violence toward others, and possibly the needs for intervention to reduce such violence, suggests that such violence is a prominent concern. That does not mean that the evaluator assumes a high risk to his personal safety in conducting such evaluations. Nevertheless, it is appropriate to consider such risk and take certain precautions. These are discussed in the next chapter.

## Collateral Information: Need and Strategies

Collateral information, in the form of records and third party interviews, is needed for several reasons in FMHA risk assessment. It is a source of information that can be considered

separate and valuable in its own right (see Heilbrun et al., 2008; Melton et al., 2007). But it is also essential to accurately complete any specialized risk assessment tool that is used. The PCL-R requires access to records in order to inform the ratings; evaluators are cautioned against using the PCL-R if they do not have such records (Hare, 1991). Other specialized measures (e.g., the HCR-20 and the VRAG) incorporate a PCL score, and therefore need records' access in order to use them.

The strategy for collecting records might be summed up as follows: The more the better—within reason. Records documenting a history of violent or other antisocial behavior may be drawn from multiple domains. These include mental health treatment records; medical records; jail, prison, and secure hospital records; arrest history (including juvenile history); arrest report; victim/witness statements; school records; and employment history. Obtaining such records will add valuable information from different sources, although the evaluator should keep in mind that many records are not independent. "Histories" of an individual are often taken from previous histories obtained on a prior admission or different commitment—in this way, inaccuracies can become repeated sufficiently often that they become accepted with confidence.

Often, however, it is not possible to obtain records that are sufficiently comprehensive to address the important domains in FMHA risk assessment. Interviews with third parties can help to "fill the gaps" in these cases. In addition, such interviews can provide information that is somewhat independent of records—and independent of one another, when interviewees are selected according to who is most knowledgeable within independent domains (Kraemer et al., 2003). The remainder of this section will discuss strategies for managing certain kinds of problems that can limit the accuracy of information obtained through collateral interviews (see Table 4.1).

**Table 4.1** | Problems Limiting Collateral Interview Accuracy in Violence Risk Assessment and Suggested Strategies for Problem Management (adapted from Heilbrun, Warren, & Picarello, 2003)

| Problem | Problem Description | Suggested Strategy |
|---|---|---|
| Reluctance to Participate | • Apprehensive About Process<br>• Concerned about Personal Consequences of Participating<br>• Unwilling to have Information Attributed | • Notification of Purpose and Limits of Confidentiality<br>• Informed About Voluntary Nature of Participation<br>• Informed That Unattributed Information Cannot be Used |
| Bias | • Lack of Impartiality<br>• Strong Positive or Negative Feelings about the Litigant<br>• Preference for Outcome | • Consider Potential Bias From the Beginning<br>• May be Assessed Near the End of the Interview With Question Such as "What Do You Think Should Happen With ____?"<br>• Third Party Information Should be Obtained From Multiple Sources, Particularly When Bias Is Suspected<br>• Conclusions Should be Developed from Trends Rather Than Single-Source Observations |
| Lack of Specific Expertise | • Without Training or Experience in Specific Area (e.g., Psychopathology, Substance Abuse) | • Initial Questions Should Elicit Broad Observations (What Did the Defendant Say? Do? Act Like?) |

**4**
chapter

*(Continued)*

| Problem | Problem Description | Suggested Strategy |
|---|---|---|
| | • May not Detect Subtle Indicators of Disorder or Capacity Being Assessed | • Later Questions Should Focus on Specific, Preselected Observations of Symptoms and Behavior (Did the Individual Show X? Act like Y?)<br><br>• No Questions Should Elicit Conclusions (Was he Angry?) |
| Suggestibility | • May be Prone to Influence from Leading Questions | • Initial Questions Should Elicit Broad Observations (What did the Defendant Say? Do? Act Like?)<br><br>• Later Questions Should Focus On Specific, Preselected Observations of Symptoms and Behavior (Did the Individual Show X? Act Like Y?)<br><br>• Allows Comparison Between Uncontaminated Description (Given With Little Guidance From the Interviewer) With More Specific but Possibly Less Impartial Version Given When Asked About Specific Relevant Areas |
| Memory Loss | • May have Difficulty Remembering Relevant Details if Saw Individual Only Once<br><br>• Influences Such as Stress, Different Races of Observer and Individual, Gun Focus, and Other Factors Interfering with Eyewitness Identification may Operate | • Beginning with General Questions and Moving to More Specific Areas<br><br>• Providing Nonsensitive Memory Aids, Such as Date and Location |

# Reluctance to Participate

There are a number of reasons why a potential collateral interviewee might not want to provide information about the individual being evaluated. Even after receiving a clear notification of the purpose of the interview, the prospective interviewee might not understand his or her role. It differs from that of a witness, as this individual will not be expected to appear before the court and testify in the presence of the evaluee. For some of the same reasons that potential witnesses are reluctant to testify, however, some third party interviewees are disinclined to provide information—fear of possible consequences to their own safety and that of their family, reluctance to provide information that might "harm" the evaluee, and concern about being involved with a legal proceeding in any way. These concerns may be heightened when potential interviewees are informed that they cannot provide information without attribution. Their names and the basis for their knowledge must be cited in the report, along with the information that they provide, so it is clear to the reader where this information was obtained.

> **BEST PRACTICE**
> Notify potential collateral interviewees of the purpose of the interview and limits of confidentiality, including that they must be cited as the source of any information provided for your evaluation.

Preceding the collateral interview, the evaluator must give the individual notification of the purposes of the interview and a description of the limits on confidentiality. Following receipt of this information, the individual's consent to participation in the interview is required to continue. For individuals who are not legally able to provide consent to participate in a process with potentially major life consequences (e.g., minors, those with a legal guardian), the evaluator should obtain their agreement to participate (their assent) along with the permission of the parent or guardian who is responsible for making legal decisions on their behalf. Obtaining this agreement must reflect the fully voluntary nature of participating in a collateral interview. Those who do not agree to participate under the conditions described in the notification (e.g., the interviewee will be identified and quoted, with this information cited in the report) must be informed that the interview cannot be conducted.

**4**
chapter

## Bias

Violence risk is a sensitive area. The behavior targeted in such assessments is by definition harmful to others. The risk of bias in one direction or another should be considered in the same way for collateral interviewees that it is for the individual being evaluated. Evaluators are seeking observations rather than opinions from interviewees. Nevertheless, collateral interviewee bias can result in the underreporting (or overreporting) of both violent acts and the seriousness of these acts. Both strong feelings about the individual being evaluated and a preference for a certain outcome of legal proceedings can contribute to potential bias in a collateral interview participant. Just as the response style of the individual being evaluated is considered in all cases, so should the evaluator be attentive to possible underreporting or overreporting of collateral interviewees. Consistent responses in only one direction are one suggestion of potential bias. A second indicator involves the response to questions asked at the end of the interview, such as, "What do you think should happen with _____ (the individual being evaluated)? What would be the best way for this to turn out?"

Even when bias appears strongly likely, it can be difficult to determine which aspects of the information provided by this interviewee should be deemphasized or discarded. There is a better basis for this decision when information has been obtained from multiple third parties. As in other aspects of FMHA, the evaluator should avoid drawing conclusions on the basis of a single source—but the single collateral interview in which there is suspicion of substantial bias may ultimately provide no contribution whatsoever to the overall information obtained in the evaluation.

## Lack of Specific Experience

Many of the individuals who are interviewed in the course of gathering third party information do not have training in psychopathology. In one sense, this is not at all problematic. Evaluators should be seeking observations, not conclusions, from interviewees. Moreover, in FMHA risk assessment, these observations are often responses to questions about threats and aggression. Consequently, the lack of training in psychopathology may present no difficulty when questions are asked appropriately and focused particularly upon observations of behaviors relevant to offending and violent behavior.

> **BEWARE**
> Be cautious of influencing responses and soliciting conclusions from collateral interviewees.

However, lack of training and experience in psychopathology can be problematic if the individual being interviewed is asked about some of the more subtle behavioral indicators of disturbance. This is especially relevant when the interviewee has not had much contact with the individual being evaluated (e.g., when the third party is a victim or witness). To address this problem, Table 4.1 describes a pattern of questioning from broad questions posed early in the interview ("What happened? How did he act? What did she say?") to more specific questions targeting the possible observations of particular symptoms or behavior. This order is important. Asking more specific questions initially would create the risk of "shaping" the account by providing subtle cues. Almost without exception, the evaluator should avoid asking for conclusions from collateral interviewees. Occasional exceptions might be made when (a) the person being interviewed is quite familiar with the individual being evaluated, and thus has experience interpreting the meaning of that individual's behavior; or (b) the interviewee has both experience with the evaluee and professional expertise in drawing such conclusions.

## Suggestibility

Individuals without specific expertise in the domains of interest in FMHA risk assessment may be prone to being "led" in a third party interview. But this phenomenon is hardly limited to this particular class of interviewees. Anyone being interviewed has the potential to be influenced into providing information that is inaccurate; some individuals (even when avoiding deliberate distortions and trying to be accurate) are particularly susceptible to such influence. Substantial scientific literature clearly demonstrates that "memories" can be created through suggestion (see, e.g., Loftus, 1992, 1997), and that the accuracy of eyewitness accounts is affected by influences such as weapon focus and cross-racial recognition (Wells & Olson, 2003). Both criminal investigations and legal proceedings have mechanisms designed to avoid undue influence on suggestibility. It is important that evaluators do the same, beginning with an open-ended approach to questioning and moving to more specifically focused questions that might steer responses *only after the initial information is obtained*. Among other things, this allows a comparison of the "unguided" and "potentially guided" versions. Substantial discrepancies between these versions should raise concerns about whether the latter version has been unduly influenced by the questions that were asked.

## Memory Loss

There is an important distinction between individuals who are interviewed based on their brief observations of the evaluee, and those being questioned due to extensive and perhaps long-standing experience with the evaluee. In the former kind of interview, the challenges presented by suggestibility and limitations upon memory are substantial—and have been observed in the scientific literature for decades. In the latter kind of interview, questions based on patterns of behavior that have been observed over a period of months or longer do not call for the same kind of specific detail, and focus on a much larger set of observations. Evaluators should be particularly attentive to the problem of memory loss when asking detailed questions of individuals whose exposure to the individual was limited (and perhaps occurred under highly stressful conditions). In managing this problem, evaluators can provide nonsensitive cues (information that has no direct bearing on the account of behavior relevant to violence, but might facilitate more accurate recall by allowing the individual to focus). For instance, the evaluator might ask for a description of minor, nonsensitive details on the day of the alleged act (e.g., "When did you wake up?", "What did you eat for breakfast?", "Where did you go afterward?"). These questions gauge the interviewee's capacity to recall and report details about the relevant time, but are not "sensitive" in that they are neither incriminating nor blameworthy. As much as possible, however, evaluators should avoid providing cues that are directly relevant to violent behavior and hence exacerbate the risk of "shaping" the account that is provided by the interviewee.

**BEST PRACTICE**
Use "nonsensitive" cues for facilitating an interviewee's recall, but do not provide cues directly relevant to violent behavior.

# Ethical Issues and Conflicts in Contacts With Evaluees, Attorneys, and Collateral Informants

A number of ethical issues and conflicts may arise as part of an evaluator's contact with evaluees, attorneys, and collateral informants. These involve consent and notification, contact with attorneys, and limits on confidentiality.

## Consent and Notification

When an FMHA risk assessment is ordered by the court, the individual does not have a legal right to refuse to participate. This should be recognized in the process preceding the evaluation. Asking defendants to consent to participating in a court-ordered evaluation is like asking citizens to consent to paying taxes. Both may decline to do so, but this choice is not meaningful given the adverse consequences for declining. Accordingly, defendants should not be asked to provide informed consent to participate in court-ordered evaluations—but should be given a full notification of the nature, purpose, possible uses, and limits on confidentiality associated with the evaluation, as well as be informed of the distinction between the forensic role and a therapeutic relationship. This notification should include a description of the consequences for declining to participate in a court-ordered evaluation, which may include the defendant's inability to present the results of another (defense-requested) evaluation in a hearing or trial, as well as the possibility that the report will be written but less well informed than it would be with the individual's participation (Melton et al., 2007).

For other (attorney-requested) evaluations or interviews with collaterals, however, informed consent is necessary. The suggested elements of the "informed" part of the process do not differ from the notification of purpose described in the previous paragraph.

Potential collateral interviewees should be provided with information on these points, and also informed that the information they provide will be documented in the report and attributed to them by name.

## Attorney Contact

The nature of the ethical issues arising in the course of contact with attorneys is somewhat different. In many jurisdictions, attorneys who represent criminal defendants can provide authorization for an evaluation of their clients who are unable to provide autonomous consent (e.g., minors, individuals with appointed guardians). (Evaluators should be aware of the relevant law and practice in their particular settings.) "Consent" is not precisely what is needed when an evaluator is discussing a potential FMHA risk assessment with an attorney, but an open discussion about the evaluator's training, experience, specific expertise, approach to such evaluations, and fees is important before the decision to proceed can be made. The evaluator providing an attorney with an updated CV will often address several of these points without the need for additional discussion.

One other point regarding interactions with attorneys is particularly salient in risk assessment evaluations. The nature of the information collected and the conclusions reached—targeting violent and otherwise antisocial behavior, the risk of repeating it, and sometimes the needed interventions to reduce such risk—is particularly sensitive. Describing previous acts of violence can create the risk of legal prejudice, in the sense that a court or jury may overvalue the importance of one particular act and diminish the value of multiple signs and patterns of behavior that are more important in risk assessment. It is important to emphasize to attorneys that sensitive information will necessarily be gathered and described, but the evaluator

**BEST PRACTICE**
Emphasize to attorneys the cumulative nature of information to be obtained during the risk assessment.

will be responsible for highlighting the cumulative nature of the evidence as it relates to conclusions. This is particularly important in order to anticipate and avoid possible requests from counsel to rephrase or delete specific information gathered in the risk assessment. Evaluators must very seriously consider the important balance between providing the consumer with the information that goes into drawing the conclusions, but accentuating the collective state of this information—the patterns that emerge—rather than the individual acts. Having considered that balance, evaluators can then explain the inclusion of specific information to attorneys. Attorneys seeking an alternative approach can then decide to pursue that if so inclined.

## Limits on Confidentiality

The applicable law that is relevant to how FMHA risk assessment will be used, or may be used, varies across jurisdictions and by type of evaluation. These limits should be quite clear to the evaluator before beginning the evaluation. Clarification may require consultation with the attorney; for instance, some attorneys do not want any results written until the findings are first discussed with them. If the attorney has requested the evaluation and thus controls whether the results will be presented in evidence, this is an appropriate request. It does present a certain challenge—the interpretation of data and drawing of conclusions is often facilitated by the process of writing, so evaluators facing such a request from counsel must be certain that the information they provide orally does indeed represent a comprehensive summary of their findings and conclusions.

**BEST PRACTICE**
Clarify the limits on confidentiality, including the circumstances in which information can be used, before beginning the evaluation process.

One of the most important reasons for clear limits on confidentiality is so these limits can be presented in the notification of purpose or informed consent process. A second reason involves identifying the contexts in which this information will (or might) be used, but also noting the circumstances under which it will not. FMHA risk assessment is subject to being used for the legal purposes for which it is intended. It may become part of a record that can be accessed for legal purposes in future litigation. However, the use of such material for extralegal purposes (e.g., professional conferences, publications, comments to the media) should be avoided unless subsequent (postlitigation) authorizations are provided by those affected, including the individual evaluated and possibly the attorney and the court. The use of such materials for professional training purposes may constitute an exception, if such materials are genuinely used for training purposes only, this exception is authorized from the beginning, and the materials are treated with the same privacy protections that apply to other sensitive materials in a training site. The evaluator should decide before beginning the evaluation how she will handle reports of behavior that are relevant to risk assessment but also legally relevant and undocumented. For example, an evaluee who reports committing a violent crime for which he was never charged is providing information that is both relevant to the present evaluation and also germane to other interests (e.g., police investigations, prosecution, and possibly appeals if another individual was convicted of this offense). The evaluee may also provide information suggesting that he presents a significant risk for harming an identified third party. The author's own preference for dealing with such material involves following the guideline provided by the American Bar Association:

> *Duty of evaluator to disclose information concerning defendant's present mental condition that was not the subject of the evaluation.* If in the course of any evaluation, the mental health or mental retardation professional concludes that defendant may be mentally incompetent to stand trial, presents an imminent risk of serious danger to another person, is imminently suicidal, or otherwise needs emergency intervention, the evluator should notify defendant's attorney. If the evaluation was initiated by the

court or prosecution, the evaluator should also notify the court. (American Bar Association *Criminal Justice Mental Health Standard* 7-3.2(b), 1989, p. 73, italics in original)

Using this guideline, the evaluator would disclose certain information under specific circumstances to the evaluee's attorney and at times to the court. Information relevant to unsolved crimes or offenses for which another defendant has been convicted is not among these, although disclosure of this information to the individual's attorney would not be problematic if the evaluator was in doubt.

## Conclusion

Preparing for an FMHA risk assessment involves a number of considerations which have been discussed in this chapter. Clarity of purpose and communication are key aspects of such preparation. The evaluator must take distinct steps with the attorney (if that person has made the referral), the individual being evaluated, and those who might serve as collateral interviewees. When preparation is done properly, it establishes a solid foundation for proceeding with data collection, to which we turn to in the next chapter.

**4**
chapter

# Data Collection | 5

After preparation for the risk assessment, the next important stage of the evaluation involves collecting the necessary information. This chapter will cover the various aspects of data collection in FMHA risk assessment. The conventional sources of information used in FMHA include interview with the individual being evaluated, psychological testing, specialized testing, interviews with collateral observers, and review of records. This chapter will discuss each of these, focusing on their respective applications to risk assessment.

## Interview(s) With Evaluee

The depth and extensiveness of the interview depends on whether a specialized risk assessment tool will be used as part of the evaluation.

### With a Risk Assessment Tool

A risk assessment tool that is well validated and a good fit for the present evaluation will provide a great deal of valuable data relevant to an opinion about risk level. It will also offer an overview of risk-relevant needs, if that is part of the evaluation's purpose. In so doing, it will use risk factors and protective factors that have already been selected for their relationship to the target behavior of interest. Accordingly, the major functions of the interview when the risk assessment includes a specialized tool are to obtain information

1. permitting cross-checking of sources, particularly the consistency of information provided using the specialized tool and the interview;

2. concerning risk-relevant characteristics or circumstances that are substantially different for the evaluee at present than previously;

3. that the specialized tool does not provide (e.g., situational influences, pattern of violent vs. nonviolent behavior in high-risk situations); and

4. that will "individualize" the assessment of risk.

## Without a Risk Assessment Tool

There are cases in which a specialized tool is not used. Best practice in FMHA risk assessment generally requires that such a tool, when available, be employed as part of the evaluation. But there are some populations and legal questions for which a well-validated tool is not yet available. There are other instances in which the administration of a specialized tool is unsuccessful; an evaluee who declines to participate in the part of the evaluation in which the tool is administered, or provides inaccurate information, has effectively removed the specialized tool from application. Under these circumstances, the evaluator must adopt a strategy that compensates for the loss of valuable information that would have been obtained from the tool itself.

The role of the interview under these circumstances is broader and more important. First, the evaluator must consider whether it is possible to render an opinion about risk under these circumstances. If the answer is a qualified "yes," then the evaluation strategy may still need revision. Rather than drawing a conclusion about the individual's risk level relative to others in known groups, the evaluator may instead focus on the risk factors and protective factors applicable to the evaluee. Using such an approach, the functions of the interview *when the evaluation does not include a specialized risk tool* include 1–4 listed two paragraphs earlier. They also include obtaining information

5. about applicable risk factors and protective factors, and their present status as applied to this individual;

6. addressing how each dynamic risk factor might be diminished through intervention; and

7. how the individual is likely to respond to such intervention.

These steps (5–7) provide information that is particularly individualized. They might be used even during evaluations in which a specialized tool is included. But without such a tool, the predominant focus of the risk assessment may become primarily on individualized factors. These steps will be recognized as part of the anamnestic approach to risk assessment discussed in this book and elsewhere (e.g., Melton, Petrila, Poythress, & Slobogin, 2007).

There are also considerations that apply broadly in the risk assessment interview. The first involves asking the individual direct questions regarding several aspects of his experience, including his thoughts, feelings, and fantasies regarding violence, both historic and present. The second involves obtaining the individual's history of violent behavior, including the circumstances of each violent act. It might be noted, of course, that for the evaluee with a lengthy history of violent behavior, this might require a great deal of time. An extensive time commitment may not be necessary if the evaluator applies the economic concept of "diminishing returns." An evaluator in this context is seeking patterns and a broad overview when asking questions concerning violence history. If such patterns (e.g., the identification of applicable risk factors) can be identified through detailed consideration of a sample of the evaluee's violent behavior, there is no need to consider the entire history in detail.

It is important to ask questions about internal phenomena—the individual's thoughts, feeling, and fantasies relevant to violence—as well as the behavior itself. This allows the evaluator to consider the linkage between such internal phenomena and violent behavior. To what extent do violent fantasies precede violent behavior? How frequently is the individual angry but does not express this in violence? What has stopped the person from acting on these angry thoughts or feelings? Many aspects of this linkage can be considered through questions about both domains (thoughts/feelings and behavior).

The other clear advantage to this kind of questioning is *face validity*. One of the

**BEST PRACTICE**

In the interview, broadly consider the evaluee's

- thoughts, feelings, and fantasies regarding violence, both historic and present;

- violent behavior and relationship to internal phenomena; and

- experiences as a perpetrator and victim.

most important kinds of validity in forensic contexts, face validity—
the appearance of accuracy—is enhanced in FMHA risk assessment
by obtaining information that appears important to the appraisal of
violence risk.

Another interviewing consideration involves obtaining the evaluee's account of experiences as both a perpetrator and a victim.
Some individuals often attribute the responsibility for the instigation
of their own violent behavior to others, or to broader circumstances.
This might be elicited more clearly through direct questions about
their own victimization. In addition, it is relevant to know how this
individual learned to be violent. A history of physical or sexual abuse
during childhood may be linked to later violence as an adult.

## Interview Style

The particular way in which interview questions are asked can have
a significant impact. Ideally the evaluee should clearly understand
what is being asked, and respond as openly and honestly as possible
concerning what occurred. There are several ways to promote the
evaluee's understanding and limit her defensiveness. Technical language or mental health jargon should be avoided unless absolutely
necessary; asking questions about "temper" or "when you get
mad," for instance, is likely to yield clearer information than asking
about "problems with anger control." Assuming that a collateral
document (e.g., an arrest report) is invariably accurate is likely to
promote an evaluee's defensiveness if that individual has a different
perspective on how the events occurred. It is preferable to begin
questioning by using nonsensitive details only (identifying when,
where, and with whom "something" occurred, but not attributing
culpability) to identify an event. Following that, the evaluee can be
asked to respond to an open-ended query such as, "Can you tell me
what happened?" This approach is related to the evaluee's possible
perspective (mentioned in the previous section) that she was more a
victim than a perpetrator of a violent act. The evaluator need not
share this perspective. However, the initial approach to seeking
information should encourage the evaluee to provide as much information as possible. Challenging and clarifying inconsistencies come
later in the interview process—but cannot be accomplished as

effectively if the evaluator has not elicited a good deal of information from the individual about both her history of violence and her associated beliefs concerning how violent acts occurred.

The sensitive information sought in the course of risk assessment is particularly subject to being underreported. At the appropriate time, the skilled interviewer can use a "push and back off" approach. The evaluator "pushes" by challenging the individual in the face of information that is internally inconsistent (described differently in another part of the interview) or inconsistent with information from other sources. If the individual becomes angry, upset, or overly defensive in the face of such challenges, however, the evaluator can "back off"—allowing the individual to take more time, answer the question in a different way, or respond to questions on another topic. In this way, the evaluator effectively uses the pressure associated with such questioning. The absence of challenge or requests to clarify inconsistencies would mean that the evaluator is left without a valuable means of seeking accurate information. Using this approach too frequently or intensively, however, can result in the evaluee's refusal to provide further information.

It is also important to consider the emotional tone of the overall interview. Even challenges to the accuracy of the individual's self report can be delivered without hostility or a "gotcha" tone. The evaluator who continues to display a respectful approach, appears interested in the evaluee's response (however difficult the information being provided might be), and does not respond with disapproval is likely to get more information over the course of the evaluation.

Finally, the most difficult and challenging questions should be posed at the end of the evaluation process. If the individual being evaluated stops participating in the face of such difficult requests, then it would be unfortunate to have this occur when the evaluator has not yet asked less challenging questions or completed other tasks (e.g., psychological testing, specialized tools).

# Collateral Information

Two kinds of collateral information are important in FMHA risk assessment: interviews with third parties and records (Heilbrun, Warren, & Picarello, 2003). Each will be discussed in this section. The information that can be obtained from such collateral information is important for at least four reasons. *First*, it helps to inform ratings and judgments made using specialized risk assessment tools. *Second*, it is relevant to response style. Risk assessment involves obtaining information in sensitive areas that appear directly relevant to risk judgments; evaluees may perceive the reporting of information about violence as harmful to their interests, and hence be inclined toward underreporting or denial. Obtaining information from multiple collateral sources can minimize the impact of such underreporting. *Third*, it allows the evaluator to weigh the possibility of a change in personal attributes or situational influences so substantial that relying heavily on history (as specialized risk assessment tools do) would produce a misleading appraisal of current risk. (This can work in both directions. For example, an otherwise high-risk individual who is physically incapacitated as the result of an accident would present a much lower risk of harming others; a low-risk individual who feels threatened and desperate may present a much higher risk of imminent violence.) *Fourth*, obtaining collateral information allows the evaluator to individualize the assessment. It encourages language in the report that not only describes the individual's risk relative to that of others (as actuarial tools do), but also his risk relative to his own functioning at other times, as well as information that is specific to his own case.

## Review of Records

The review of records may be reasonably straightforward. When an individual is being evaluated while in a secure setting—a jail, prison, detention facility, or forensic hospital—there may be records describing recent and more distant acts of violence, arrests and convictions, and behavior in different settings (with levels of supervision ranging from the most structured, in a secure setting, to the least structured, in the community with no supervision).

Medical and mental health records are typically included in facility records as well.
These can be particularly useful if the
FMHA risk assessment includes a risk management component. Domains that are less

**BEST
PRACTICE**
Make reasonable attempts to
obtain relevant records, with
an awareness that you may
not always succeed.

likely to be readily available (at least for adults) in facility records
include juvenile, school, employment, and military records. In
some cases, the added time and effort needed to obtain such additional records may be justified. At other times, it may be preferable
to obtain some information in these areas but acknowledge that
the sought-after records would not add sufficiently to the overall
value of the documentation to justify such additional effort. Best
practice in this area calls for reasonable attempts to obtain relevant
records, but does not require that the evaluator always succeed.
Indeed, as Monahan (1993) points out, a policy that required
obtaining *all* relevant records while conducting risk assessment
would inevitably mean that evaluators would fall short in trying to
follow the policy. This would have potentially disastrous results in
*Tarasoff* or negligent release litigation, *even in cases in which risk
had been appropriately assessed* (although, tragically, the conclusion
proved to be inaccurate).

In other cases, however, obtaining relevant records can be
extremely challenging. If there is not a conveniently available
record, the evaluator can make a request for records to the
referring attorney. If possible, a request to both opposing attorneys, irrespective of who has made the referral, may be useful.
For court-ordered evaluations, the evaluator may seek an order
that specifies the provision of relevant records as part of the
evaluation.

## Interviews With Third Parties

The second collateral strategy—conducting interviews with those
who are familiar with the individual being evaluated—can supply
primary information if records are unavailable, can "fill in the gaps"
regarding information not contained in records, and can provide
another source of information against which to calibrate the consistency of information from the individual and records.

**BEST PRACTICE**
Interview collateral informants from separate domains for greatest effectiveness. Separate domains may include

● family

● friends/broader social network

● employment

● treatment/monitoring

● victims/witnesses

Selecting collateral informants who have had regular contact with the individual is important to obtain an accurate accounting of that person's current and recent violence. In the MacArthur Risk Assessment study, for instance, the report of a collateral observer was a far more sensitive indicator of the presence of violent behavior than were official records of rearrest or rehospitalization (Monahan et al., 2001). When multiple collateral informants are sought, one effective strategy is to begin with the informant who is most knowledgeable about the individual. Often this would be a close family member or partner. However, the second collateral should be the most knowledgeable observer from a different domain—a coworker or case manager, for example. Kraemer et al. (2003) have suggested that this approach to selecting the best-informed collateral observer from one domain, then the best-informed from a separate domain (rather than another well-informed observer from the same domain) is most likely to maximize the effectiveness and accuracy of collateral observations in clinical research—and, by extension, in forensic assessment.

Particular strategies for seeking information and managing problems that would distort the accuracy of collateral observations (e.g., forgetting, bias) are discussed in the next chapter. They have been described at greater length elsewhere (Heilbrun et al., 2003). Using the Kraemer et al. (2003) approach, the evaluator might consider the following domains in identifying one potential collateral from multiple contexts: *family* (of origin, current), *friends/broader social network*, *employment*, *treatment/monitoring* (case managers, probation or parole officers, therapists, jail/prison/hospital staff), and *victims/witnesses*. Obtaining access to these collateral observers can vary in difficulty from relatively minor to extreme. Contact with collateral observers such as victims or witnesses should be pursued only when both attorneys and the court have authorized it. Other observers may be unable to comply with what is effectively a request to release information if they are bound by the policies of their institution. Compliance can be facilitated if the individual being evaluated provides permission to release information. Theoretically it can also be accomplished if the collateral interview (releasing information) is authorized by a court order. However, while a court can authorize the release of information in a case at hand, it cannot compel the collateral interviewee to participate.

## Psychological Testing

Most psychological tests have little direct relationship to violence risk or risk-relevant intervention needs. This is one of the reasons for the development of a number of specialized risk assessment measures (described in the next section). However, the same might be said of the relationship between psychological testing and the functional legal capacities associated with other kinds of FMHA, which contributed to the need to develop specialized measures to assist in the evaluation of different legal questions. The respective contributions of psychological tests and specialized measures to the broader FMHA process vary somewhat across types of FMHA, as may be seen in the volumes on different topics in this series.

Nevertheless, there is a role for traditional psychological tests— those measuring personality, psychopathology, intellectual and neuropsychological functioning, and patterns of behavior. Consider the distinction made several years ago between *forensic assessment instruments*, *forensically relevant instruments*, and *clinical measures* (Heilbrun, Rogers, & Otto, 2002). Forensic assessment instruments are those developed to provide direct information about the functional legal capacities and other relevant attributes related to a specific legal question. Forensically relevant instruments are those designed to measure a construct that is frequently important, although less directly related, to legally relevant functioning. (For example, the PCL-R [Hare, 1991] and measures of response style such as the SIRS (Structured Interview of Reported

**INFO**

Psychological tests, including clinical measures as well as forensically relevant instruments, can help address questions in FMHA risk assessment.

Symptoms) [Rogers, 1992] help appraise constructs such as psychopathy and malingering that are important in different kinds of FMHA.) Finally, clinical measures are psychological tests developed for diagnostic, symptom and deficit description, and intervention-planning purposes with clinical populations.

There are certain questions that these traditional psychological tests can help to answer in FMHA risk assessment. First, it may be helpful to have an accurate description of the individual's clinical functioning. A few kinds of clinical symptoms (e.g., substance abuse) are strongly related to violence risk in a variety of populations. Other kinds of symptoms or attributes (e.g., violent fantasies, anger problems, impulsivity; see Monahan et al., 2001) may be related to violence risk in certain populations. Yet other symptoms or behaviors (e.g., medication noncompliance, delusions) may be related to violence risk for certain individuals.

Second, there are some psychological tests (e.g., the Minnesota Multiphasic Personality Inventory-2; Tellegan et al., 2003; the Personality Assessment Inventory; Morey, 2007; the Millon Clinical Multiaxial Inventory-III; Millon, Davis, & Millon, 1997) that include a measure of propensity for antisocial behavior, perhaps using one or two scales. Evaluators should certainly be cautious with such results, as the link between these scale results and the behavior targeted in FMHA risk assessment is often weak (or not described in the manual and related literature). But as a broader consideration, it may be useful to consider whether an individual with co-occurring psychotic and personality disorders is at greater risk for harming others when the symptoms of psychosis are active—or when they are in remission. Psychological tests can contribute to the understanding of an individual's symptoms, motivations, and patterns of thinking and behavior, within which the specific appraisal of violence risk and risk-reduction needs can be understood more meaningfully.

There are additional questions that can be addressed in part by forensically relevant instruments. Measures of recognized violence risk factors such as substance abuse, anger control, impulsivity, and violent fantasies are among those that may be particularly useful in some cases. The PCL-R (Hare, 1991) has a fairly strong track record of predicting violent reoffending and general reoffending in the community, to the extent that some (Gendreau, Goggin, & Smith, 2002) have presented data suggesting that the PCL-R is not the "unparalleled" measure of offender risk it has been considered by many in the field. But the PCL-R was developed as a measure of psychopathic personality disorder, not as a risk assessment measure, so it is somewhat ironic that it has performed so well in risk assessment. Whether it is "unparalleled" or not, however, the PCL-R is certainly one measure that is often relevant and related to the risk of future violent and general offending.

## Specialized Risk Assessment Tools

It is beyond the scope of this book to review in detail the major specialized risk assessment tools that are available for use with adults. Fortunately, such a book devoted to precisely this purpose will shortly be available (Otto & Douglas, in press), providing a description and analysis of the best specialized risk assessment tools that are now in use. Several comments are relevant to this point. First, the use of a specialized risk assessment tool is consistent with best practice in FMHA risk assessment. Such a tool should be incorporated into the assessment when it is (a) available through derivation and validation research on populations and for purposes comparable to the present risk assessment, and (b) commercially available, with usage supported by a manual describing the procedures for administration, scoring, and interpretation along with supporting research. The failure to use such a specialized risk assessment tool when these criteria are met should be justified as part of the evaluation, acknowledged as a limitation upon cross-examination, and avoided whenever possible.

It is useful, however, to consider several specialized risk assessment tools, selected because they are well developed and meet the criteria for use described in the previous paragraph. These tools are compared on 15 dimensions (see Table 5.1) in a way that might be helpful to evaluators and programs selecting a specialized tool for their own needs. The following tools, which were also reviewed in Chapter 3 with respect to their

**BEST PRACTICE**

Use a specialized risk assessment tool relevant to the particular area of risk whenever one is empirically supported and available.

chapter **5**

**Table 5.1** Comparison of COVR, HCR-20, LS/CMI, and VRAG on Relevant Dimensions for Risk Assessment

| Relevant Dimensions | COVR[1] | HCR-20[2] | LS/CMI[3] | VRAG[4] |
|---|---|---|---|---|
| Prediction | P | P | P | P |
| Validation for Prediction | 3 | 3 | 3 | 3 |
| Risk Reduction | A | P | P | A |
| Validation for Risk Reduction | N/A | 2 | 2 | N/A |
| Comprehensiveness | 2 | 3 | 3 | 2 |
| Efficiency | 3 | 2 | 2 | 3 |
| Ease of Administration | 3 | 2 | 2 | 3 |
| Predictive Utility | 3 | 3 | 3 | 3 |
| Intervention-Planning Utility | 2 | 3 | 3 | 2 |
| Decision-Making Utility | 2 | 3 | 3 | 2 |
| Communication Utility | 3 | 3 | 3 | 3 |
| Commercial Publication | P | P | P | P* |
| Available Test Manual | P | P | P | P* |
| Peer Reviewed Publication | 3 | 3 | 3 | 3 |
| Decision-Making Formula Known to Evaluator | 2 | 2 | 3 | 3 |

Notes: 1 = limited to none; 2 = partial; 3 = good to excellent; P = present; A = absent.
[1] Classification of Violence Risk (Monahan, Steadman, Appelbaum, et al., 2005);
[2] Historic-Clinical-Risk Management-20 (Webster et al., 1997); [3] Level of Service/Case Management Inventory (Andrews et al., 2004); [4] Violence Risk Appraisal Guide (Harris et al., 1993).

* Manual information contained in appendixes of books (Quinsey et al., 1998, 2006).

empirical support, are described: the COVR (Monahan, Steadman, Appelbaum, et al., 2005), the HCR-20 (Webster, Douglas, Eaves, & Hart, 1997), the LS/CMI (Andrews, Bonta, & Wormith, 2004), and the VRAG (Harris, Rice, & Quinsey, 1993). The COVR was developed for use with individuals who are psychiatrically hospitalized or considered for hospitalization, while the LS/CMI is appropriate for use with general offender populations. Neither is presently indicated for use outside of their respective domains. The HCR-20 has been validated for use in both civil and criminal populations, although it is most applicable to those in these populations who experience severe mental illness. The VRAG appears indicated for criminal populations but not presently for noncriminal populations. These differences illustrate the importance of population in helping to determine the applicability of a given tool.

As may be seen in Table 5.1, all four of these tools have been validated for making predictions. However, these tools approach such prediction differently. Both the COVR and the VRAG are actuarial tools developed only for predictive purposes, while the HCR-20 and the LS/CMI are risk-needs tools that seek to describe both risk of reoffending (including violently) and criminogenic needs/dynamic risk factors that can be targeted for risk-reduction interventions. Accordingly, only the HCR-20 and the LS/CMI are rated as to "validation for risk reduction" purposes. The "partial" rating reflects the still-limited state of risk reduction research at present, although this is changing. The COVR and VRAG are rated as less comprehensive because they are focused on prediction only. However, they are more efficient to use and easier to administer than are the risk-needs tools. The HCR-20 is a structured professional judgment tool that calls for a conclusion based on evaluator judgment in light of the evidence collected, while the other three tools are actuarial in their use of total scores to yield levels of risk. A recent review suggests that good SPJ and actuarial tools are comparable in predictive accuracy (Heilbrun, Douglas & Yasuhara, in press), so all four of these tools are rated "good to excellent" in predictive utility. The intervention-planning applicability of a prediction-only tool is largely limited to the implications for intervening in consideration of good information about that individual's violence risk level. Risk-needs tools provide more information about intervention planning, including specific areas and symptoms to be targeted. The decision-making utility of each of these tools is good when the decision centers on risk of future violence. When the modification of such risk is part of the decision, however, then risk-needs tools provide more information. All four of these tools yield results that can be effectively conveyed to a decision maker—assuming that the evaluator separates the issues of risk and needs, and describes the latter only when the tool provides a basis for doing so. All are commercially available and have a supporting test manual. (The VRAG and supporting material that would otherwise go in a manual are published in appendixes in two books: Quinsey, Harris, Rice, & Cormier, 1998, and Quinsey, Harris, Rice, & Cormier, 2006.) Each is supported by a number of studies published in peer-reviewed journals, as described in Chapter 3. The "decision-making formulas" employed by the LS/CMI and the VRAG, respectively, are relatively straightforward to understand and easy to communicate. It is more complex with the COVR, as the conclusion is reached through multiple iterations of decision tree analysis. This is a methodologically sophisticated approach to analyzing large data sets. But it also requires the evaluator to be aware of how the analytic procedures work, and it cannot be replicated by hand. It is also more complex with the HCR-20, but for a different reason: there is no formula. To be aware of what has influenced her decision, the evaluator must think carefully about how she considered each of the various factors in reaching a final conclusion.

## Safety Guidelines

Conducting an FMHA violence risk assessment does not necessarily create any greater risk to the personal safety of the evaluator than does any other kind of FMHA. Nonetheless, it is useful to be prudent and professional. The individuals being evaluated are involved in legal proceedings in which their risk of violence has been identified as a relevant question. This alone should justify the observation of guidelines

**BEWARE**
Take precautions to protect your personal safety when interviewing evaluees.

developed to minimize risk to the personal safety of the evaluator. These guidelines are described in this section.

- *The clinician should be familiar with safety policies applicable to the practice site.* Often such evaluations are conducted in secure facilities—prisons, jails, detention centers, and secure hospitals. Such facilities have policies that are designed to avoid escape and interpersonal violence. Staff members should be appropriately trained in such policies. Evaluators who enter the facility for the purpose of conducting a single evaluation, however, should ensure that they are sufficiently knowledgeable about such policies to comply with them. Moreover, visiting evaluators should cooperate with security staff and proactively seek clarification on questions related to security.

- *Evaluators should question staff about the condition of the individual to be evaluated before meeting with that individual.* Staff members who provide security and treatment in secure facilities are likely to know whether an individual has recently behaved in a way that might raise concerns about the usual FMHA-necessary conditions involving privacy, quiet, and freedom from distraction. Individuals who are prone to become easily agitated and angry, who have been involved in recent fights, or who have been isolated for disciplinary or protective purposes are among those who might be evaluated under somewhat different conditions (or at another time), depending upon the recommendations of knowledgeable staff members.

- *Evaluation conditions should be modified to minimize the risk to evaluator, staff, and the individual being evaluated when particular problems are apparent.* When discussion with staff members or other indicators suggest that the individual may easily become upset, angry, or aggressive, the first question

chapter **5**

to be considered is whether to postpone the
evaluation. This should be seriously considered. It can
also be presented to the individual at the beginning of
the evaluation (e.g., "If you need to stop for any
reason, let me know and we can do that."). If the
evaluator decides to proceed, then conditions should
reflect adequate protective measures. Staff should be
available to assist in the event that a client becomes
agitated or aggressive. If the individual is restrained
through mechanical means such as cuffs or leg
restraints, then it may be useful to leave these in place.
If the policy of the facility is such that the individual
must remain within close proximity of a staff member,
it may be possible to negotiate an arrangement in
which there is visual contact from a distance that does
not allow the content of conversation to be overheard.
Multiple evaluators may be used if this is feasible.

- *The notification describing the purpose of the evaluation
  should address safety as well.* Evaluees are routinely
  notified about the reason for an evaluation, the kinds
  of tasks that will be involved, and the limits of
  confidentiality. When indicated, the evaluator can
  expand this notification to include the comment that
  some of the procedures may be difficult or upsetting.
  This can be handled through breaks, working on a
  different topic as necessary, or even rescheduling the
  evaluation—but it is important in the beginning to
  emphasize that all of these are available so both
  evaluee and evaluator can be safe. It makes a
  difference, of course, *why* the individual might
  become violent. An individual who is impulsive and
  easily agitated (for instance, an impulsive young man
  of limited intellectual functioning who is upset with
  his attorney because the lawyer "can't get me out of
  here") differs from an individual who is delusionally
  convinced that the evaluator is an alien intent on

harming him. A jail inmate intent on taking a hostage differs from an individual who is extremely frightened of prison incarceration that could result from the legal proceedings associated with the evaluation. Some awareness of the individual's history and current functioning can help the evaluator make an informed decision about which particular safety precautions are appropriate.

- *The contents of the room should be examined for possible weapons.* The typical office contains many items that could be used for weapons. Lamps, telephone cords, pens, letter openers, bottles, chairs, computer printers, picture frames, and other metal or glass items that can be twisted or broken to produce sharp edges are among the most common items that can be used as a weapon to produce serious or lethal injury. A safe space should contain none of these items. Use of a cellular phone rather than a desk phone may facilitate communication without providing a potential weapon.

- *The room should be large enough to permit a comfortable distance between the evaluator and the individual being evaluated, and the evaluator should not sit between that individual and the door* (Otto & Borum, 1997). Some individuals are bothered by close quarters. In addition, having a reasonable amount of intervening space also gives the evaluator more time to respond if the individual becomes agitated. Someone who becomes very upset and walks out of the room has created only a minor inconvenience for the evaluator, so this kind of response is not discouraged if it is necessary. Allowing the individual to sit next to the door makes it easy for that individual to leave.

- *Establish a prearranged signal with staff to communicate an emergency in a nonobvious way* (e.g., "Please reschedule my next appointment for Friday the 13th at noon" ; Otto & Borum, 1997). In some settings, the evaluator can easily summon staff through pressing a "panic button" or otherwise signaling an emergency. In others, however, this is not feasible. Outside of a secure setting, it may be necessary to have someone else contact assistance. Having a prearranged signal like this can alert office staff to respond to a potential emergency without informing the individual being evaluated.

- *Screen for weapons in emergency settings* (Otto & Borum, 1997). In facilities that provide assessment and treatment services to acutely disturbed individuals, it is important to ensure that individuals who enter "off the street" do not bring weapons in. This is particularly important when such individuals have not been observed by staff earlier, so they may also be intoxicated or under the influence of drugs.

- *Evaluators should receive training in noninjurious restraint techniques and other aggression management approaches.* Such techniques are designed to allow an evaluator, in the course of a physical attack by an individual, to restrain that individual for a brief period of time while minimizing the risk of serious injury to either. If assistance does not arrive shortly, such techniques may not suffice to prevent injury. But their use can be effective if the conditions of the evaluation have been established so that assistance from staff can be summoned quickly.

- *Evaluators should be polite and respectful at all times, even when confronting a client with sensitive material or inconsistencies.* As much as the substance of difficult, challenging questions, it may be the emotional tone to which some evaluees respond when the questions convey a feeling of "gotcha." Maintaining a respectful tone at all times, even when individuals are responding in a way that is internally inconsistent or clearly at odds with other information, will convey that even difficult or problematic material will be treated with respect and without rancor or hostility.

- *The emotional tone of confrontation should convey a polite request for help in understanding* (the mildly perplexed investigator approach). Saving the "reconciling of inconsistencies" for the end of the evaluation is a good strategy, as this is often the stage at which confrontation is inevitable. Adverse responses can be limited even at this stage by continuing to convey a respectful tone, but adding an element of puzzlement at such inconsistencies.

## Conclusion

This chapter has addressed a variety of considerations in the data collection phase of FMHA risk assessment. Interviews, collateral interviews, psychological testing, and specialized risk assessment tools are all important elements in this kind of evaluation. The description of data collection provided in this chapter should make it clear that risk assessment in the context of FMHA does differ in some important respects from risk assessment provided for other purposes. The same may be said for the interpretation phase of FMHA risk assessment, to which we now turn.

# Interpretation | 6

This chapter will address the interpretation of data gathered in FMHA risk assessment. Since the interpretation process for FMHA broadly has been described in detail elsewhere (Heilbrun, Grisso, & Goldstein, 2008; Melton, Petrila, Poythress, & Slobogin, 2007), this book focuses primarily on matters that are specific to risk assessment. The chapter will begin with the interpretation of specialized risk assessment tools and a description of the "adjusted actuarial" debate, along with a proposed resolution. Next, it will discuss the integration of results obtained from a specialized risk assessment tool with information obtained from other sources, including interview, third party information, and psychological testing that is not specialized for risk assessment. Examination of the recent debate concerning the applicability of actuarial results to individual cases (see, e.g., Hart, Michie, & Cooke, 2007; cf. Harris & Rice, 2007; Mossman, 2007; see also Heilbrun, Douglas, & Yasuhara, in press) will follow, and a perspective on its implications for best practice in this area will be offered. The two final sections of this chapter will discuss the limitations on the accuracy of FMHA risk assessment, and the logic of the interpretation of results.

## Interpreting Specialized Tools

The number of specialized risk assessment tools that have been developed during the last 15 years is remarkable. The development of such specialized tools has been one of the most important influences in promoting evidence-based practice in this area. Using such a specialized tool is clearly consistent with best practice—assuming that an appropriate tool is available.

Beginning with the assumption that such an appropriate tool is available, its selection is an important and often challenging step in the evaluation process that should not be treated lightly. Interpretation of a specialized risk assessment cannot be done meaningfully when a poor tool is used—or when a good tool is used inappropriately.

## Congruence With Population, Nature of Behavior, and Outcome Period

The appropriate use of a tool involves a certain congruence between the population on which it was developed and the individual being evaluated. Such congruence should also extend to the nature of the outcome, with the validated outcome(s) associated with the specialized tool reasonably consistent with the nature of the behavior and the outcome period described by the legal question.

The interpretation of the results of the specialized tool should be completed according to the manual that accompanies it. Even though population and outcome congruence between the specialized tool and the immediate case is important, it is never feasible to expect a tool to map identically onto the legal question. For example, the COVR (Monahan et al., 2005) was derived and validated on individuals from a population consisting largely of civilly committed individuals. It would be appropriate for use in the evaluation of an individual for civil commitment. Yet this legal decision may focus most on an individual's short-term risk of harming others if not hospitalized, perhaps over the course of the next week. The 6-month outcome period over which the COVR was validated is probably a longer period than most courts would consider for the immediate decision. Moreover, there are other components to the legal decision on civil commitment (typically declining voluntary hospitalization and risk of harm to self) that the COVR does not address.

Accordingly, it is important that a specialized tool be interpreted in a way that clearly describes the nature of the harm to others and period of time over which the risk is calculated. This will never be fully synonymous with all elements of the legal question from a specific jurisdiction. Other sources of information can be used to increase this congruence as part of the final opinion.

## Confidence Intervals

Another important aspect of the interpretation of specialized tools is confidence intervals. Actuarial tools that yield levels of risk in predicting who will be violent should also have confidence intervals associated with the mean for each level. These confidence intervals must be considered in the interpretation. The forensic clinician can be reasonably certain that narrow 95% confidence intervals reflect a mean that is representative of the group's risk of violence, while wider confidence intervals make such a mean less representative. Consider the difference, for instance, between a tool that identifies a given individual as "high risk" based on a score placing him in a category in which 50% of the individuals committed a violent act (with a 95% confidence interval of .48–.52), and a second tool which yields a similar score and conclusion with a 95% confidence interval of .30–.70. The figure of .50 could be used meaningfully in the first instance. It would be less meaningful in the second. The level of precision in the interpretation of a specialized risk assessment tool is important, and can be reflected in part by including the confidence intervals surrounding the means of risk categories. The failure of those who develop specialized tools to specify 95% confidence intervals when appropriate is a serious shortcoming; forensic clinicians should be quite cautious about using such tools.

**6**
chapter

## Reference Groups

Yet another consideration is reference groups. "Compared to whom" and "compared to what" are important questions in the design and interpretation of supporting research. They are also important questions in the interpretation of specialized tools. The tool may yield a series of risk categories that allow comparisons within the same group,

**BEWARE**
Be cautious in using tools for which 95% confidence intervals have not been specified.

ranging from lowest to highest. In this scenario, the comparison groups are others within the same population. One of the useful aspects of anchoring each risk category in an "average" outcome is how this facilitates the comparison of an individual in the population being assessed with individuals from other populations for whom base rates of offending or violence have been published. Specialized tools typically do not provide this kind of comparison group. However, it can help in interpreting the meaning of risk assessment results when a certain risk category is compared with the outcomes of those in other groups.

## Actuarial Versus Structured Professional Judgment Approaches

The next important point in the interpretation of specialized tools concerns actuarial versus SPJ approaches. As described in detail earlier in this book, research to date comparing these two approaches has not yielded a clear advantage to either in terms of outcome accuracy. Whether a specialized tool is actuarial or SPJ, it is important to interpret consistently with the manual. There is one respect in which a good actuarial tool can be interpreted more clearly. One of the assumptions behind SPJ tools is that the evaluator, having assessed the presence of the risk factors described in the tool, can then draw a conclusion using professional judgment concerning the risk level presented by the evaluee. But only through research on the actuarial application of risk factors can the tool's manual specify the quantitative meaning of high, intermediate, and low risk—including both means and confidence intervals. So this particular anchor, with its capacity to relate the present findings to the outcomes of other groups, is not available with SPJ tools unless research has also investigated the application of its risk factors in a quantitative way.

## The "Adjusted Actuarial" Debate and Resolution

The debate on what has been called "adjusted actuarial" centers around whether the results of actuarial risk assessment should be modified in light of other considerations. There are two ways in which this has been debated: adjusting the score or the associated risk level of the actuarial tool at the scoring stage, and adjusting the meaning of the tool's results at the interpretation stage. Each will be discussed in this section.

The idea that an evaluator can meaningfully adjust the score is very problematic for several reasons. First, actuarial tools are designed to be used in a specified way. This involves combining the item scores to yield a total that is interpreted using an established algorithm. They were not designed to be scored or totaled using the kind of "clinical adjustment" that is contemplated in this debate; doing so would call into question the meaning of the adjusted score. Second, changing the score in this manner to some extent substitutes clinical judgment for the actuarial algorithm, something that is likely to result in a consistent albeit modest disadvantage to accuracy in the long term. Finally, unless the evaluator is open about what she has done, the result may appear to be actuarial when it is not. The conclusion is straightforward: This kind of "actuarial adjustment" *during the scoring* should never be done; to do so would violate best practice standards.

The other approach to "adjusting" the actuarial tool involves the interpretation of results. This is a more complex matter. On one hand, consistently changing the "yield" of an actuarial tool will reduce the predictive accuracy of that measure. On the other hand, FMHA risk assessment involves more than the prediction of how someone will behave. The approach taken in this book involves treats this debate in the context of FMHA more broadly. One of the important principles of forensic assessment involves the use of multiple sources of information and gauging consistency across sources (Heilbrun, 2001; Melton et al., 2007). No single source of information is treated as entirely persuasive, and final opinions depend upon the integration of information across sources. So "adjusting" the results of an actuarial tool *at the interpretation stage* is a legitimate consideration. Indeed, it is less that the results of the tool are "adjusted" than that they are

**6**
chapter

**BEWARE**
Never adjust the results of an actuarial tool at the scoring stage.

weighed less heavily, for reasons that can and should be articulated, in the context of the final opinions. For example, an evaluator using the COVR might observe that the conclusion yielded by this tool placed the individual in the second lowest of five risk categories. However, the evaluator might conclude that the short-term risk for violence toward others is somewhat higher, considering the individual's specific threats toward a third party, access to that individual following discharge from hospitalization, and access to means of harming that person. *How much higher* the risk would be could not be quantified, of course.

# Integrating Other Data

What other sources of information are important in FMHA risk assessment? How might this information suggest a deviation from the results of a specialized tool noted in the previous section? This section discusses the data to be drawn from the interview, from third party information (including records and collateral interviews), and from psychological testing (that is not specialized for risk assessment).

## Interview

The interview can be used for several important purposes. These include the following.

### ANAMNESTIC ASSESSMENT

Anamnestic assessment involves the individual's description of relevant behavior (e.g., violence, offending) and the circumstances surrounding each event. Who was involved? What occurred? What led up to it and followed it? Was it accompanied by the consumption of alcohol or drugs? Prescription medication? Where did it occur? Gathering this kind of information can help to create a detailed history, which provides a context within which other information regarding violence risk and risk reduction can be interpreted (see Melton et al., 2007).

## CROSS-CHECKING FACTUAL INFORMATION
In the course of a risk assessment, the individual being evaluated provides factual information regarding history, as well as present and historical information regarding thinking, feeling, motivation, decision making, and behavior. It is worthwhile for the evaluator to ask similar questions at different stages in the evaluation. This can help gauge the internal consistency and potential accuracy of the information provided by the evaluee.

## HIGH-RISK SITUATIONS AND RESPONSES
The concept of the "high-risk situation," often incorporating the presence of multiple risk factors applicable to the individual being evaluated, is useful in risk assessment. But questions about the individual's exposure to high-risk situations, and her behavior in such situations, are not routinely asked in the administration of specialized risk tools. It is quite useful to have the individual describe her behavior in such situations. Is it consistently violent? If not, what distinguishes those instances in which the individual behaves violently from those in which she does not? Does the individual recognize the concept of "high-risk situation"? Is that individual able to avoid some such situations by early recognition of the triggers? The answers to these types of questions can supplement the risk assessment context, but can also provide useful information regarding the individual's response to interventions that seek to reduce risk.

## PROTECTIVE FACTORS AND RISK FACTORS
Related to the individual's understanding of the concept of high-risk situations, it is useful to inquire about the evaluee's view of the influences that incline him toward behaving violently, and those that keep him from doing so. Very often such questions do not

yield valuable information. Many individuals evaluated for violence risk are not particularly insightful concerning the influences that affect their own violent behavior. However, this line of questioning can provide useful information concerning an individual's mental and emotional functioning related to violence risk, and his potential for favorable response to certain kinds of interventions.

## Third Party Information

One of the particularly valuable aspects of collateral interviews involves the opportunity to ask a knowledgeable observer the same questions (described in the last subsection) that were asked to the evaluee. This allows cross-checking, identifies points of inconsistency, and suggests areas that will either be unclear (because of such inconsistency) or need even further input. When multiple third parties are interviewed, it appears best to select individuals who are reasonably knowledgeable about the individual being evaluated—but from different domains (e.g., family, work, programs) (Kraemer et al., 2003). This facilitates the interpretation of information from different sources by maximizing the novel contribution of each source.

Official records have been treated as a necessary and valuable source of information in both risk assessment and FMHA, so they clearly will provide an important contribution to FMHA risk assessment. Such official records (typically a result of arrest or hospitalization for a violent act) underestimate the incidence of violent behavior in the United States (Steadman et al., 1998), so it should not be assumed that violence did not occur if it was not reflected in an official record. Nevertheless, records are particularly valuable for confirming events (such as arrests) reported by other sources, offering a description of violence that occurred while the individual was incarcerated or hospitalized, and providing documentation of the impact of various interventions to reduce the risk of imminent violence.

## Psychological Testing

It is sometimes useful to obtain further information about an individual that may be considered as additional context or sources of hypotheses. For instance, the evaluator might administer a broadband, objective personality inventory with scales sensitive to response style (e.g., the MMPI, MCMI, or PAI) to develop additional hypotheses concerning the individual's functioning and risk factors. Such hypotheses would be subject to verification or refutation through other sources of information. Alternatively, the evaluator might administer psychological testing to obtain further information concerning risk factor(s) that seem applicable to this individual. Some possible factors follow.

**BEST PRACTICE**

Consider additional psychological testing for factors such as

- substance abuse,
- psychopathy,
- anger, and
- intellectual functioning.

## SUBSTANCE ABUSE

One of the most powerful risk factors for violence across a number of different populations is "substance abuse." Specifics details are required for maximal understanding of its impact on the evaluee's violence risk. What are the substances of choice? The frequency and level of use? Differential impact on violence risk? Is the individual involved in selling as well as using drugs? Many of these questions might be answered through the administration of additional testing using a measure of drug and alcohol use.

## PSYCHOPATHY

Another powerful risk factor, psychopathy (as measured by the PCL-R), is a standard part of several risk assessment tools, including the VRAG and the HCR-20. A discussion of psychopathy and associated tools is included in Chapter 3.

## ANGER

Anger is an important variable because it functions as a risk factor for violence in some cases, and also because there are direct implications for intervention. If it appears that the individual has a problem with anger, this may be described much more clearly through the administration of a somewhat specialized measure to tap this domain (e.g., the Novaco Anger Scale and Provocation Inventory; Novaco, 2003).

## INTELLECTUAL FUNCTIONING

Intellectual functioning may be a variable assessed to determine whether (a) particular weaknesses in comprehension of social

chapter **6**

situations and verbal skills limit the evaluee's behavioral reper-
toire, making violence more likely because more adaptive
responses are less feasible; or (b) it can be treated as a potential
strength that might compensate for the presence of other risk factors. There may also be other reasons to formally assess an individual's intellectual functioning. Like other domains listed in this
subsection, it does not appear to be an area that best practice
would dictate should be assessed routinely. However, when
earlier-stage screening suggests that it may be important to the individual's violent risk, such formal assessment can be very helpful.

## Is Actuarial Risk Assessment Applicable to Individuals?

The recent debate within the field concerning whether actuarial
measures can be interpreted with respect to the individual (see
Hart et al., 2007; cf. Harris & Rice, 2007; Mossman, 2007) has
implications for the interpretation of actuarial tools and other
sources of information discussed in this chapter. As discussed earlier, one of the important points made by Hart and colleagues
(2007) concerns confidence intervals. Another one of their major
themes, however, concerns the application of an actuarial measure (which is, by definition, developed using nomothetic research
and tracking the outcomes of groups of individuals) to an individual. They described the applicability of confidence intervals to
individual cases using Wilson's formula (Wilson, 1927). This may
not be a meaningful use of this formula, as the authors them-
selves acknowledge. There should be no disagreement that the
size of confidence intervals is inversely related to the size of the
sample. For instance, a coin flipped 100,000 times will have a
very narrow confidence interval around the probability of
"heads" (.50), while a coin flipped 10 times will have a much
wider confidence interval. What this suggests is twofold: (a) the
larger the derivation and validation samples for an actuarial tool,
the better; and (b) one can be less confident about the outcome
of an actuarial measure when applied to a small number of cases
than when applied to a large number. These are concerns that are

appropriately handled in the interpretation and risk communication phases of FMHA risk assessment.

This does not mean, however, that actuarial tools cannot be applied to individuals. It is appropriate to handle concerns about applicability of any data in risk assessment through interpretation and conveying of limitations (to be discussed further in the next section). However, if one views the assessment of risk as a series of evaluations to be conducted by most evaluators, and a series of decisions to be made by most courts, then the implication that we are making only a single decision is misleading. We seek strategies to maximize our accuracy in both the single case (through conventional FMHA strategies involving multiple sources of data, cross-checking for consistency, considering source credibility, and drawing conclusions best supported by these data) and across multiple cases (including the use of specialized risk assessment tools that are either actuarial or SPJ).

But there are implications for the derivation and application of actuarial tools to groups. One such implication involves the combination of sources very frequently present in FMHA: both nomothetic and idiographic information are valuable, for different reasons, and both merit inclusion. Furthermore, the language used to convey the results of actuarial risk assessment may be a particular consideration. Typically this involves a choice between the use of frequencies (e.g., "1 of 20 such individuals") and probabilities (e.g., "5% likely"). This will be discussed further in the next chapter.

**chapter 6**

# Limitations on Risk Assessment Accuracy

## Prediction

Despite the substantial advances in risk assessment over the last two decades, there remain some clear limitations on the predictive accuracy associated with FMHA risk assessment.

Particular influences that can impair predictive accuracy are as follows:

- *No appropriate specialized risk assessment tool.* The strongest single contributor to an accurate prediction of future violent

**BEST PRACTICE**

Be sure that limitations on predictive accuracy are incorporated into the interpretation, conveyed in the report, and acknowledged as part of expert testimony.

behavior appears to be a specialized risk assessment tool. The absence of such a tool within the evaluation methods is likely to limit predictive accuracy substantially.

- *Specialized tool has limited fit with the legal question.* A specialized predictive tool may be available but not map well onto the contours of the legal question. If the evaluator is aware of this limited congruence but decides to include the measure nonetheless, it is very important to make clear what the results of the tool suggest and how these results do (and do not) help inform the legal decision.

- *Specialized tool has wide confidence intervals and/or overlapping risk categories.* The question is how well a mean score within a category, or the category itself, represents the individual being evaluated. When confidence intervals are narrow and categories are mutually exclusive, then neither imposes limitations on predictive accuracy. Wider confidence intervals make the mean score of a category less meaningful in representing the individual; overlapping categories make the categorical risk assignment less certain.

- *Limited sources of information do not allow consistent cross-checking.* Like any FMHA, the quality of a risk assessment depends partly on the number, nature, and credibility of sources. Having fewer good sources means that evaluators are limited in one of the most basic aspects of forensic assessment—the cross-checking of consistency using multiple sources. This applies to specialized tools as well as other aspects of the evaluation. For instance, both the VRAG and the HCR-20 use the PCL-R score as one of their items; the PCL-R cannot be completed without review of a collateral record.

## Risk Reduction

Research on interventions to reduce violence risk is less advanced than research
describing the predictive parameters of violence. It is reasonable to assume that the
reduction in the number and intensity of dynamic risk factors will
result in a decreased risk of violence and violent offending. This
is also consistent with the risk, need, and responsivity model
(Andrews, Bonta, & Hoge, 1990; Andrews, Bonta, & Wormith,
2006). However, with a few noteworthy exceptions (e.g., multi-
systemic therapy with juveniles), the empirical basis for predicting
the outcomes of specific interventions in order to reduce the risk
of violence is quite limited. Accordingly, the best practice strategy
at present involves identifying dynamic risk factors that are applicable to the individual, suggesting interventions that would be
appropriate in addressing each, and using care about implying that
this strategy *will* reduce risk.

**BEWARE**
Avoid making
claims sug-
gesting that interventions
will necessarily result in risk
reduction.

One way of considering the possibility that such interventions
will reduce risk involves obtaining historical information concerning interventions that have been delivered to date—and the individual's response. If the intervention has never been delivered, or has
been provided in a lower intensity or more limited duration than
might be indicated, then this may not be helpful. Nevertheless, the
evaluator should attempt to obtain such information. Without such
a reasonable attempt, the evaluator must not only observe the limits on opinions regarding risk reduction but explain why there was
no attempt to obtain potentially relevant information.

**6**
chapter

# Accounting for the Logic of FMHA Risk Assessment

There is a particular logic to the way in which forensic clinicians
interpret data and link this interpretation to their conclusions. One
important aspect of FMHA is to make this logic clear, so the reader
can follow the progression from data to conclusions (Committee
for Specialty Guidelines for Forensic Psychologists, 1991). Several
elements of this reasoning are as follows.

## Hypotheses

The most basic hypothesis in a risk assessment concerns the individual's level of risk for the specified target behavior. It is more appropriate to frame such a hypothesis in the terms applicable to a specialized tool (e.g., low, moderate, or high risk) than in legal terms, as the question of whether an individual presents a sufficiently high risk to justify the legal decision being considered is a variation on the ultimate issue debate. This is discussed in detail in Chapter 7. Additional hypotheses may be posed regarding the impact of situational variables, the potential response to relevant interventions, and other considerations that are relevant to the legal question(s) being evaluated.

## Weight of the Evidence From Multiple Sources

The weight assigned to the findings from a specialized risk assessment tool, particularly when it is a "good fit" for the evaluation being conducted, should be substantial. But it may be considerably diminished if it contains information that cannot be supported in its factual accuracy through multiple sources. Such sources are also used to provide information not available from a specialized risk tool, possibly including applicable risk factors that are not described by the specialized tool—or dynamic risk factors if a specialized measure employing static factors is used. Ultimately, the general FMHA principle that calls for data to be evaluated for consistency across multiple sources is as important in risk assessment as it is in other kinds of forensic assessment.

## Correcting for Response Style

One specific influence that may distort the accuracy of risk assessment data involves response style. Most often, the evaluator should be concerned with the underreporting of relevant history, behavior, motivation, and decision making that would, if reported accurately, elevate the evaluee's risk. This must be approached thoughtfully, as many of the specialized response style measures have focused on detecting the opposite kind of responding—the exaggeration of symptoms or deficits. One potential measure for defensive responding can be obtained using a validity scale for defensiveness from a psychological test such as the MMPI, MCMI, or PAI. However, it seems likely that the sensitivity of many of the questions posed during a risk assessment promotes a more pervasive tendency to underreport, minimize, justify, and rationalize. The prudent evaluator should recognize this influence and compensate for it through the use of third party interviews and record review.

## Considering Situational As Well As Individual Variables

Unless the forensic clinician uses a tool that explicitly incorporates the influence of situation into the appraisal of risk, there is likely to be a substantial gap in the information yielded by such a tool. This gap must be filled. Situations can have a powerful impact on risk; tools that are validated on violence risk in the community, for example, do not yield results that are generalizable to a structured setting such as a correctional facility or a hospital. Moreover, there are a variety of specific circumstances that may apply to the broader situation involving "living in the community." A thorough review of the situational influences on the individual's violent behavior is thus an important aspect of the FMHA risk assessment.

## Incorporating Protective Factors and Information About Not Behaving Violently

Even high-risk individuals with significant histories of violence toward others are not violent in much of their behavior. The focus of a risk assessment should not be exclusively on violence. There is important information embedded in an individual's history of nonviolent behavior, particularly under circumstances that are high risk for that individual. Some specialized risk assessment tools now incorporate protective factors, which can facilitate the formal assessment of this kind of influence. The LS/CMI, for example, allows the user to specify factors that appear to influence the individual to refrain from offending. Another approach to gathering such relevant information involves asking detailed questions (of both the evaluee and of collateral observers) about events that could have culminated in violence—but did not.

### Megargee's "Algebra of Aggression"

One useful approach for conveying the general logic of violence risk assessment involves the "algebra of aggression" developed by Edwin Megargee (1982). He proposed four broad influences on the likelihood that an individual would behave aggressively: instigation, inhibition, habit strength, and situations. In Megargee's view, instigation (the sum of influences inclining one toward behaving aggressively) and inhibition (the sum of influences inclining one against behaving aggressively) could be understood as primarily individual influences, albeit in opposing directions, while habit strength and situation are historic and contextual variables, respectively. One advantage to using this description is its simplicity. It describes influences of different kinds, makes it clear that violence risk is conceptualized as multidetermined, and conveys the broad logic by which the evaluator seeks to describe the individual as part of the risk assessment.

## Conclusion

This chapter has addressed the influences on the interpretation of data that are collected in the course of FMHA violence risk assessment. Interpretation is a crucial part of any FMHA. One of the reasons it is particularly significant in risk assessment, however, involves the availability of a number of good specialized risk assessment tools and the way in which their results are integrated with other data to yield conclusions and opinions. The interpretation of these data provides the link between the information that is collected and the conclusions that are drawn in a way that can be understood by the legal decision maker. There is one remaining step in the evaluation process—the communication of data, reasoning, and conclusions in the report and testimony—to which we turn in the final chapter.

# Report Writing and Testimony | 7

Communicating the findings of a risk assessment is a crucial final step in the overall evaluation process. This chapter will discuss the important aspects of communicating the results of a violence risk assessment in a forensic context. Both report writing and testimony will be considered. The majority of this discussion will focus on the report, however, for two reasons. First, the communication of FMHA results involves only a report in the majority of cases, with "report plus testimony" in a minority of cases (Melton, Petrila, Poythress, & Slobogin, 2007). Since the report itself will be the only evidence offered in many cases, it is particularly important that it be done properly. Second, even when expert testimony is required, the evaluator should be able to base the testimony directly on the report, which should strengthen the credibility and accuracy of the testimony considerably (Heilbrun, 2001).

The discussion will begin with the organization of the report. There are different approaches to organizing FMHA reports (see Heilbrun, Marczyk, & DeMatteo, 2002, for a number of examples). Each has strengths and weaknesses. These will be addressed in the context of the larger two-part goal: (a) to provide a product that is sufficiently comprehensive, thorough, and informative to assist the legal decision makers and attorneys when presented as evidence *without* the evaluator present; and (b) to serve as a foundation on which credible and accurate expert testimony can be based.

Next, the length of the report will be considered. There is an important balance between thoroughness and practicality when communicating the results of FMHA risk assessment. A report conveying data, conclusions, and opinions regarding an individual's risk of violent behavior must be sufficiently comprehensive to make it useful in legal proceedings as a "stand-alone" document. But there are limits on the available time and effort of all parties involved, so evaluators should strive for conciseness as well as accuracy. This chapter will offer some examples of the length and depth of reports that seem indicated in various kinds of risk assessment.

There is some information that should *not* be included in FMHA risk assessment. Typically an evaluator would exclude information that was either irrelevant or prejudicial, but neither of these is a straightforward decision. The considerations of legal relevance and what might be sufficiently prejudicial to justify exclusions will both be addressed.

The question of reporting raw testing data (whether psychological testing or specialized risk assessment) is particularly salient in the present context. Some of the content contained in specialized risk tools could influence decision makers to respond emotionally, acting on anger or fear, *even when the overall risk appraisal may call for a different conclusion* when all the data are considered. Evaluators must make every attempt to ensure that the overall risk appraisal is guided by all relevant data, not just those that are most conspicuous. However, evaluators also have an obligation to be open about the nature of the information obtained, and the process by which they reasoned toward conclusions and opinions. The notion of balancing will again be used to guide this discussion.

The overall process in which relevant data are gathered, combined in ways that are empirically supported, and used in drawing conclusions through the evaluator's clearly described reasoning has been widely cited and well accepted in FMHA (see, e.g., Grisso, 2003; Melton et al., 2007; Morse, 2008). Accordingly, this will be the approach used when integrating the risk assessment into the larger context of the FMHA. Since there are often other legal questions that are also addressed in a forensic evaluation in which risk assessment is a part, the integration of risk assessment data into the evaluation addressing multiple criteria will be further considered using this sequencing approach (data → reasoning → conclusions → opinions).

There are some specific considerations in risk communication that are particularly relevant to report writing and testimony. In particular, the use of nomothetic versus individualized language, frequencies versus probabilities, and confidence intervals will be discussed. Each is important in conveying results as accurately as possible—and in a way that is least likely to be misunderstood by the decision maker.

Expert testimony on risk assessment has an additional set of challenges. Even assuming the existence of a strong foundation provided by the evaluation and report, experts face the daunting task of conveying information in an area that is subject to distortion through misunderstanding of basic data/reasoning and challenges during cross-examination.

Whether the forensic evaluator should answer the ultimate legal question is a topic that has been debated widely in forensic psychology and forensic psychiatry for 30 years, and is addressed in some detail in the first book in this series (Heilbrun, Grisso, & Goldstein, 2008). Doubtless this debate will continue. But the present book makes the observation that the debate has particular importance in risk assessment evaluations, given the vagueness of legal constructs that are often applied (e.g., "dangerousness," "threat to public safety"). Whether the forensic evaluator decides or declines to answer the ultimate legal question on risk assessment, this chapter will offer a series of points that are vital for promoting understanding of the results of the kind of risk assessments described in this book—whether these results are presented in the report, or in both the report and testimony.

## Organizing the Report: Different Approaches

Both the author's professional experience and the relevant research (Borum & Grisso, 1996; Christy, Douglas, Otto, & Petrila, 2004; Felthous & Gunn, 1999; Hecker & Steinberg, 2002; Heilbrun & Collins, 1995; Heilbrun et al., 2002; Lander & Heilbrun, in press; Nicholson & Norwood, 2000; Petrella & Poythress, 1983; Skeem & Golding, 1998; Tolman & Mullendore, 2003) suggest three approaches to documenting the results of FMHA risk assessment. These can be identified as (a) the brief report, (b) the narrative report, and (c) the sectioned report. A brief description and discussion of the advantages and disadvantages of each will follow.

## The Brief Report

This is a report that provides only limited documentation of what was evaluated, using what sources, providing what data, and combined toward conclusions by what reasoning. It may be as simple as a checklist often used in civil commitment proceedings, in which the evaluator provides only a summary judgment on each of several relevant points (see Pinals & Mossman, in preparation). It may be conveyed in a short (one- to two-page) report or a comparably short letter to the judge.

Perhaps the only advantage of the short report is practicality. It requires relatively little time to write or dictate. However, even this apparent advantage may be illusory. Any FMHA report submitted as part of a legal proceeding may result in the evaluator being subpoenaed to provide expert testimony. Some such testimony is inevitable—when opposing counsel plans to vigorously challenge the findings and minimize the impact of the opinion, for instance, there is likely to be a contested hearing. However, there are also instances in which opposing counsel may subpoena an evaluating expert because the written report itself is insufficient, confusing, or lacking in credibility. This is more likely with a brief report, because while it can convey the conclusions and recommendations of the evaluator, it cannot reasonably document the basis on which these are made. Such occasions can quickly diminish the "net savings" of time for the forensic clinician, who must add travel and waiting time to the preparation and testimony time necessary to participate in a hearing or trial.

**BEWARE**
Be aware of the disadvantages of the brief report, especially involving challenges from opposing counsel.

The disadvantages of the brief report are much clearer. Some of the most prominent problems with FMHA reports as forensic psychology and forensic psychiatry began to mature in the 1970s and 1980s are reflected in Grisso's critiques of such evaluations in the first edition of *Evaluating Competencies* (1986). Two of the major criticisms of forensic evaluations at the time, he observed, were *insufficiency* and *incredibility*—reports did not provide enough information to allow the reader to learn about the data acquired in the evaluation, and understand the reasoning that linked this data to the conclusions. This is particularly important in the adversarial context. Opposing counsel preparing to challenge the opinions of the forensic clinician will find it more difficult if she cannot determine the basis for these opinions. (Of course, in another respect, the job of opposing counsel is simplified when the expert's report is brief. The attorney can point out the essentials that are lacking in such a report, diminishing the perceived credibility of the expert in so doing.) It is also noteworthy that a brief report may attempt to hide the reality that relatively little time and effort went into the entire assessment process, a weakness that can be readily uncovered in deposition or cross-examination. Brief reports may also present a problem if the expert is called to testify. The information contained in any report should serve as the foundation for the expert's testimony. When a brief report is submitted, it may be necessary to prepare another document to "remind" the expert of all of the data and findings. This other document, if obtained by opposing counsel through discovery, can contribute to the impression that the evaluator was withholding significant information in writing the initial report.

Best practice in risk assessment FMHA will typically include an interview with the evaluee, collateral information (records and interviews with third parties), and often psychological testing. When a specialized risk assessment tool has been developed and validated on the fitting population and for reasons consistent with the present purpose, then the inclusion of such a tool is consistent with best practice. The presentation of a good, relevant, multi-sourced history is particularly important in providing the context for appraising the risk for future violent behavior and possibly the indicated approaches to reducing this risk. It is exceedingly unlikely that this information could be described, or even synopsized meaningfully, in a brief report.

**7**
chapter

**BEWARE**
Narrative reports are usually not conducive to clearly presenting conclusions or serving as a basis for expert testimony.

## The Narrative Report

This is a report of greater length. The organizational structure is such that it appears to be written or dictated from notes, and so is more often used by forensic clinicians who primarily use interviews and record reviews. Such reports do have the potential strength of thoroughness, as they often contain an extensive account of information provided by the individual being evaluated as well as information from other sources.

The major disadvantage to this form of report is its organization. In presenting a great deal of information in a way that does not lend itself to locating specific points or synthesizing data into conclusions, such a report is difficult to read and hard to use as a foundation for expert testimony. It is analogous to obtaining a great deal of information and then dropping it all into a file drawer. The information is all there—but try finding a specific item (particularly within the time constraints associated with testimony under cross-examination).

It may be that this kind of report structure works better for experts with excellent memory, who can produce accurate, organized, and complete responses on cross-examination even when they do not have the "raw data" easily accessible. (The author has one highly-respected colleague who does not take *anything* onto the stand when he testifies!) But this is not a good strategy for most forensic psychologists and psychiatrists. When testifying about the results of FMHA risk assessment, it can be crucial to report even small details accurately. What is needed, then, is a reporting structure that promotes the description of data and their analysis through clearly described reasoning toward a conclusion, and provides a way of quickly locating specific factual material in varying domains.

## The Sectioned Report

This approach to report writing involves the use of multiple sections, with headings and subheadings to guide the reader. The particular headings generally in an FMHA report have been discussed elsewhere (Heilbrun et al., 2008; Melton et al., 2007; Simon & Gold, 2004a). Table 7.1. lists the typical headings and corresponding information.

**Table 7.1**   Typical Organization of a Sectioned Report

| Section Heading | Content |
|---|---|
| *Identifying Information* | Regarding Both the Individual Being Evaluated and the Purpose of the Evaluation, Including the Relevant Legal Question(s) and the Referral Source |
| *Procedures* | Including Details Regarding Interviews with the Individual Being Evaluated and Third Parties, Specific Documents Reviewed, Particular Psychological Tests and Specialized Tools Administered, and the Notification of Purpose or Obtaining of Informed Consent |
| *Relevant History* | Focused Particularly on the Domains Related to the Legal Question and Functional Legal Capacities |
| *Current Clinical Condition* | A Description of the Individual's Clinical Functioning, Considered Broadly to Include Personality and Behavioral Characteristics, with Particular Focus on Symptoms and Characteristics Potentially Relevant to the Legal Question and Functional Legal Capacities |
| *Functional Legal Capacities* | Which Vary According to the Legal Question; in FMHA Risk Assessment, this Section Might be Entitled "Violence Risk Assessment" or "Reoffense Risk Assessment" |
| *Conclusions and Recommendations* | A Description of the Conclusions and Recommendations Linked Directly to the Functional Legal Capacities Identified in the First Section of the Report |

There are additional options for sections using this report structure. Some evaluators, for example, prefer to use a section entitled "Analysis" or "Reasoning" that appears between "Functional Legal Capacities" and "Conclusions." This section explicitly documents the evaluator's reasoning that links the data to the conclusions. The alternative is to include such reasoning in the "Functional Legal Capacities" section, or to write a "Conclusions" section that includes both reasoning and specific conclusions. Several additional options are discussed in the next section.

There are multiple advantages to using this structure for an FMHA risk assessment report. First, the structure is sufficiently flexible to describe the evaluation of more than one legal question. This is important because violence risk assessment is often one part of a larger legal question (e.g., civil commitment) or a separate, second issue (e.g., insanity at the time of the offense and meeting criteria for involuntary hospitalization). Second, the sectioned report is highly organized. Like a structured interview or test, it creates the demand for certain information by displaying the domain in which that information occurs. Third, it facilitates the quick location of particular information within the body of the report. This is helpful to the reader (particularly the judge or opposing counsel), and also quite useful to the forensic clinician when he is asked a very specific question on cross-examination. Fourth, it facilitates the description of separate sources of information, which promotes a better understanding of what was obtained through interview, collateral interviews, record review, and administration of psychological testing and specialized tools. Since FMHA risk assessment should include a specialized tool whenever feasible, the sectioned report allows the reader to see the results obtained from this tool—and also to determine how these results contributed to the evaluator's final conclusions.

The sectioned report structure does not have significant disadvantages. It promotes the kind of thorough, clear, multi-sourced FMHA using data → reasoning → conclusions that is a hallmark of best practice. When risk assessment is considered in the course of litigation, it should be framed within the same parameters as FMHA addressing other legal questions; the sectioned report facilitates this.

**BEST PRACTICE**

Consider using a sectioned report to clearly convey the links between data, reasoning, and conclusions.

# Specialized Sections: Executive Summary, Diagnosis, Testing

FMHA risk assessment reports sometimes include three additional features. Sections pro-viding an executive summary of the report's

findings, describing a particular diagnosis, and separately document-ing the results of psychological and specialized testing will be briefly discussed next.

## EXECUTIVE SUMMARY

Some forensic clinicians place an executive summary at the begin-ning of the report. This differs from the practice of inserting a summary prior to the conclusions section, where the reader would encounter it after reviewing the entire report. The executive sum-mary placed at the beginning of the report invites the reader to review it prior to (and perhaps in place of) the full report. This is not recommended. A reader wishing to review the conclusions without reading the body of the report can do so easily by simply reading the final section. However, there is no need for the foren-sic clinician to explicitly collaborate in this practice. The FMHA risk assessment sectioned report is sequenced to provide the pur-pose, procedures, findings, reasoning, and conclusions necessary to convey the elements of the risk being appraised. It is impossible to convey much of this information meaningfully in a brief report, let alone through a single paragraph that would constitute an exec-utive summary.

## USE OF DIAGNOSIS

The use of diagnosis in FMHA has been debated at length (see, e.g., Melton et al., 2007; Morse, 2008; but cf. Simon & Gold, 2004b). Even those who advocate the use of diagnosis seem to recognize its limitations in FMHA generally, including the oft-cited *DSM* (Diagnostic and Statistical Manual of Mental Disorders) caution that diagnostic information "will be misused or misunderstood . . . because of the imperfect fit between the questions of ultimate con-cern to the law and the information contained in a clinical diagno-sis" (American Psychiatric Association, 2000, pp. xxxii–xxxiii).

**BEWARE**
Clinical diagnoses are limited in their direct relevance to risk assessment.

Such "imperfect fit" is particularly pronounced when the risk of violence is being appraised. Certain kinds of personality disorders (e.g., antisocial personality disorder and psychopathy) are relevant to violence risk while others are not, and serious mental illness may be either a mild risk factor or a protective factor, depending upon the comparison group (see Monahan et al., 2001; Quinsey Harris, Rice, & Cormier, 2006). If diagnosis is used and cited in a separate section of the report, it is important that the forensic clinician recognize the role and limitations of diagnosis in risk assessment—and describe them clearly in the report.

## TESTING RESULTS AND ATTRIBUTION STYLE

The question of whether testing results are cited in a distinct section of the report depends upon the forensic clinician's preference for attribution of information by source. Such attribution may be "line by line" or "paragraph by paragraph." Suppose, for example, the forensic clinician was describing the individual's history of temper problems, including fighting and threats, as part of the larger risk assessment. The evaluator appropriately obtained information from the individual himself, from two collateral informants, and from a review of records, including one hospitalization and two juvenile placements. In a line-by-line attribution style, the forensic clinician would first give the evaluee's description of his temper problems, making sure this information was attributed to the evaluee himself. Immediately following would be the accounts of the collateral informants. Then the relevant information from the hospital and placement records would be provided. This style allows the reader to see the results of multiple sources regarding the same question, and to gauge the consistency of information across sources.

By contrast, the paragraph-by-paragraph attribution style would begin with a full account of the evaluee's self-reported violence history. Since all the information in the paragraph is from the same source, there is no need to repeatedly preface responses described in this paragraph with "according to Mr. X." That can be made clear at the beginning of the paragraph or the section. Then, after Mr. X's version was described in its entirety, the evaluator would document the accounts of the collateral informants. The information from the records would follow, preceded with some indication of their source. Each different source would have its own paragraph(s).

The line-by-line attribution style has the advantage of placing information on a specific point from multiple sources together. The reader can more easily gauge consistency and identify sources of discrepancy, which is particularly important if the evaluee himself is inclined to underreport (or overreport) symptoms or behaviors. However, this style is more laborious to use in writing and more difficult to read. The interspersing of qualifiers such as "he said," "she reported," and "the records reflect" must be constant. It is much easier, by contrast, to read the evaluee's version, followed by a separate paragraph on the collateral's version, and another on the records. However, this paragraph-by-paragraph attribution style leaves it largely to the reader to compare specific responses and gauge consistency across responses.

An evaluator who included a separate section on psychological testing would very probably be using paragraph-by-paragraph attribution. Indeed, some blending of these styles is virtually inevitable even for the forensic clinician who chooses the line-by-line style. The many specific elements of clinical functioning, for example, make it virtually impossible to isolate each and describe the contribution of the various sources. But it is feasible to separate the sources of information quite distinctly in a report by describing the results of each in a separate section. Best practice in FMHA risk assessment does not clearly point toward one style or the other; this decision should be made in light of the evaluator's awareness of the strengths and limitations of each attribution style.

## Completeness Versus Efficiency

This section comments on the balance between thoroughness and conciseness, and between completeness and practicality. A reasonable description of the purpose, procedures, data, interpretation, and reasoning toward conclusions cannot be provided in an "executive summary" or a brief, one- or two-page report. It is clearly outside the scope of best practice to attempt to communicate the results of an FMHA risk assessment in a report this brief. It is more difficult, however, to address the questions on the thoroughness/completeness side of this balance. Is there an ideal length (or an ideal range) for the report? Is it possible for a report to be so long and detailed that it becomes problematic?

The first guideline in addressing these questions is functionality. The report should be sufficiently long so that the purpose, procedures, data, interpretation, and reasoning toward conclusions noted in the previous paragraph are clear to the reader when the evaluator is not present. If there are unanswered questions in any of these areas, the report should be longer. This does not mean that the reader must be convinced by the report; in an adversarial system, this would be an impossible demand. But the forensic clinician should not have to offer significant additional information regarding procedures, findings, or reasoning during expert testimony. If that occurs, then the report was not sufficiently comprehensive.

The second guideline invokes the economic principle of diminishing returns. It is important to make the factual point, support it with information from multiple sources whenever possible, and then move on. If the report contains language that is repetitive or otherwise adds little to the point being communicated, then it should be more concise. This is a deceptively important point. When the essential message is surrounded by unnecessary verbiage, it is simply harder to identify.

A third guideline draws upon the twin pillars of evidence law—relevance and reliability. The information contained in an FMHA risk assessment report should be relevant to the broad process of risk assessment. This need not be taken too literally, as the description of a person's functioning when she is *not* violent can be quite important. But it is the evaluator's responsibility to provide the needed interpretation and reasoning to relate this information to the prediction and risk reduction questions. The reliability (by which the law means both psychometric reliability and validity) of various sources of information used in FMHA risk assessment cannot always be gauged. For instance, there is no empirical, scientific way to quantify the reliability and validity of sources such as the interview of the individual, interviews of third parties, and various records. The use of multiple sources is one way in which this problem is managed. But it is also important—and within the parameters of best practice—to select and use psychological tests and specialized measures that have sound psychometric properties and have been validated for the immediate purpose for which they are being used (Heilbrun, Rogers, & Otto, 2002).

Finally, there is the question of practicality. Best practice does not require a tome. Even reports as short as five to six pages (single-spaced) can address the important aspects of FMHA risk assessment for certain questions. The more focused the question, the more feasible a report of moderate

> **BEST PRACTICE**
>
> Guidelines for a balanced approach to report writing include the following:
>
> ● *Functionality:* Does it adequately describe the evaluation's purpose, procedures, data, interpretation, and reasoning toward conclusions?
>
> ● *Conciseness:* Is the report repetitive or does it include unnecessary verbiage?
>
> ● *Relevance and Reliability:* Is the information relevant to the evaluation and from reliable sources?
>
> ● *Practicality:* Does the report address the important aspects in a focused manner?

length. For instance, the forensic clinician addressing the question of "future dangerousness" in the context of capital sentencing should properly confine the scope of this appraisal to the defendant's future behavior while incarcerated, since the report will not be used at sentencing unless the alternatives are life incarceration or execution (see Cunningham, in press). However, the outcome period over which this appraisal is focused might be very lengthy. These two considerations would have competing effects on the needed length and thoroughness of the risk appraisal in this context.

# Information That Should Not Be Included

The general assumption in FMHA, including risk assessment, is that information reviewed and obtained in the course of the assessment should be included in the report. Of course, this assumption is subject to the considerations of functionality, relevance, and

**BEWARE**
Strategically withholding information is inconsistent with ethical guidelines and best practice.

practicality discussed in the previous section. So perhaps it would be most accurate to say that anything used or obtained in the course of the assessment could be described in detail in the report, subject to the evaluator's discretion.

Information should not be withheld strategically, however. An evaluator should not fail to cite relevant information in appropriate detail because such information might be grist for opposing counsel's mill. Such strategic withholding might explain an extensive evaluation that is documented only by a brief, conclusory report. Such a failure to document the sources, data, and reasoning that underlie one's conclusions is grossly inconsistent with the letter and spirit of specialized ethical guidelines in forensic psychology (Committee on Ethical Guidelines for Forensic Psychologists, 1991) and forensic psychiatry (American Academy of Psychiatry and the Law, 2005), and thus inconsistent with best practice in FMHA risk assessment.

However, there are occasionally additional considerations beyond functionality, relevance, and practicality. One of the most important is whether specific information would be prejudicial to a litigant in a way that is beyond the scope of the referral question. This does not mean, of course, that an evaluator who concludes that a defendant is at high risk for future violence should refrain from expressing that conclusion because it might harm the defendant's interests. Nor does it mean that the evaluator should decline to document the data and reasoning that underlie this conclusion. However, there are certain kinds of information that could harm the defendant in a way that is beyond the scope of a good risk assessment. It is this kind of information that must be treated very carefully in how it is conveyed.

Two examples may be helpful. First, suppose that a forensic clinician who regularly evaluates juveniles on the legal questions of transfer and commitment routinely asks these youths about owning, carrying, and using any kind of weapon, as well as involvement in selling drugs. In a particular case, assume further that a 16-year-old male being evaluated for transfer to criminal court on charges of armed robbery reports that for 6 months last year he regularly carried a gun for protection because he was selling drugs. The offense history obtained from the juvenile court indicates that this youth has another set of charges (weapon possession and possession of cocaine with intent to distribute) that have not yet been adjudicated. Under these circumstances, quoting the youth directly regarding carrying a gun and selling drugs could have the unintended consequence of providing information prejudicial to that youth's legal interests in the other case. The forensic clinician in this case might resolve this with a compromise. Information concerning weapon possession and drug selling is relevant to a risk assessment and hence should not be excluded—but it can be conveyed in language sufficiently general so it does not clearly apply to the acts with which the youth is charged in the other case.

A second example concerns specific language that might be highly inflammatory. Suppose the (white) youth in the example just cited indicated that he had targeted his robbery victim because that individual was African American. That is relevant information in a risk assessment. But if the youth conveyed this in an explicit, highly offensive way characterized by the use of multiple racial slurs, then quoting him could have the effect of unnecessarily angering a legal decision maker. Conveying this information could involve balancing relevance and importance against the risk of unnecessarily prejudicing the defendant's interests, perhaps yielding an approach in which the evaluator conveys the essence of the information but in less graphic language.

## Reporting Test Data

Some description of the data from any psychological test or specialized risk assessment tool is valuable. The question of the level of detail in this description involves balancing practicality and the need for reasonable disclosure. On one hand, citing the responses to a long, objective psychological test such as the MMPI or the MCMI is impractical and contributes little to understanding the meaning of these results. On the other hand, when a measure is shorter and the items are summed in a straightforward fashion to determine risk level, it might be feasible or even desirable to note which individual items are rated affirmatively.

All testing data are subject to disclosure through court order, if obtained by opposing counsel. Hence, the process of rating or scoring individual items, combining them into scales when indicated, and interpreting the results should be open and transparent. But opposing counsel does not necessarily have the time or resources to obtain information in this way. The best practice regarding the reporting of testing data, therefore, should provide sufficient information to allow the consumer to determine the nature of the data collected and how they were interpreted.

# The Progression From Data to Interpretation to Opinion

Data in FMHA risk assessment should be gathered using approaches and considerations used in other FMHAs (Appelbaum & Gutheil, 2007; Heilbrun et al., 2008; Melton et al., 2007). History of relevant behavior, including prior events and their circumstances, should be obtained from multiple sources. This allows an individualized appraisal of risk, particularly the identification of potential risk factors and protective factors. Testing data from a specialized risk assessment tool should be obtained, as well as more standard psychological testing that may help to promote an understanding of such risk factors and protective factors.

The next step involves integrating the interpretation of data from multiple sources. Specialized risk tools are particularly valuable, and their results should be weighed heavily in the overall risk assessment. However, other considerations may affect how a specialized tool is ultimately interpreted, particularly the following:

• *Response style*. Inaccurate self-report can limit or invalidate the results of a specialized tool. Multisourced checking for factual information used in specialized tools is therefore quite important.

- *Outcomes beyond the scope of the specialized tool.* When the evaluation focuses on an outcome that is broader or narrower than that used with the specialized risk assessment tool, then additional information must be obtained to describe the influences affecting the risk of this broader (or narrower) outcome.

- *Broken leg exceptions.* In Meehl's (1957) terms, a "broken leg exception" occurs when there is a striking difference in the individual's present condition or circumstances relative to what is usual for that individual, making it misleading to apply idiographic norms (the individual's own base rates) or nomothetic norms (the base rates of those in an actuarially similar group). One example might involve an otherwise low-risk individual who had experienced extreme provocation from a particular individual, described a feasible plan to inflict serious harm on that individual, and had the immediate means to do so.

- *Situational influences.* Some risk assessment tools provide virtually no information about situational influence, a potent and often underestimated influence in risk assessment. The circumstances under which an individual is at highest risk for violence should be considered. Among other things, this may provide valuable clues to risk reduction strategies.

- *Risk reduction influences.* When the focus of the evaluation is on appraising both risk level and risk reduction strategies, but the specialized tool is prediction-oriented (e.g., the COVR or the VRAG), then additional information regarding intervention needs and responsivity is needed.

When the data have been described and interpreted, the progression to the final opinion(s) should be guided by the evaluator's reasoning. The structure used in FMHA risk assessment is important in this progression. The terms "dangerous" and "dangerousness" do not promote conceptual or empirical specificity, so "risk assessment," "risk management," and "risk reduction" are preferable. Using these latter terms facilitates the description of (a) risk factors and protective factors, (b) probability or level of risk, for (c) particular outcomes (Monahan & Steadman, 1994; National Research Council, 1989), and (d) indicated interventions to reduce risk. Final opinions need not be expressed in ultimate legal language, but they should relate directly to the scientific and clinical aspects of the FMHA's focus.

# Risk Communication

Risk communication is an important link between the results of the appraisal and the implications for decision making (Heilbrun, Dvoskin, Hart, & McNiel, 1999; Monahan & Steadman, 1996). This section discusses three particular aspects of risk communication that are relevant to how opinions are expressed.

## Nomothetic Versus Individualized Language

FMHA is ultimately about the individual, and the language used in opinions should make this clear. Yet best practice in FMHA incorporates both nomothetic data (psychological tests, specialized tools) and idiographic data. When interpreting the results of a nomothetic measure, it is appropriate to use language incorporating the larger reference group(s). This may include statements about behavior aggregated across the group (e.g., "a total of 45%–55% of such individuals were rearrested for a violent offense within 1 year of release") or the individual's rank relative to others in the group (e.g., "30% of those in this group were more likely to be arrested than individuals with scores this high"). There is no contradiction between using nomothetic language to interpret the results of such tools, and individualized language ("this individual, over this specified time period and these particular circumstances") to describe the evaluator's opinions about the evaluee.

⊙ **BEST PRACTICE**

Take care in expressing opinions about risk, considering

● nomothetic versus individualized language,

● frequencies versus probabilities, and

● confidence intervals.

## Frequencies Versus Probabilities

The results of specialized risk assessment tools, when used actuarially for predictive purposes, can be expressed in either frequencies or probabilities (see, e.g., Monahan et al., 2005). Consider the following examples:

> *Frequencies:* One in 20 individuals similar to Mr. X will commit a serious act of violence over a 12-month period if released to the community.
>
> *Probabilities:* Mr. X has a 5% likelihood of committing a serious act of violence during the next 12 months if released to the community.

These conclusions are comparable in the quantitative values they convey. Either is consistent with best practice, but there are considerations associated with the decision to use one or the other. The frequencies-based form better conveys Mr. X's status relative to the group on which the supporting research is based. However, there is also evidence that these forms of communication are not perceived as comparable, with "1 in 20" regarded as a more serious risk than "5%" (Slovic & Monahan, 1995; Slovic, Monahan, & MacGregor, 2000). There is also some debate surrounding the meaning of "5%" for an individual, particularly in the context of 95% confidence intervals (see Hart, Michie, & Cooke, 2007, but cf. Harris & Rice, 2007; Mossman, 2007). This is addressed in the next section.

**7**
chapter

## Confidence Intervals

Actuarial, prediction-oriented risk assessment tools typically employ categories of risk. There are differing numbers of such categories across tools; four (Static-99; Harris, Phenix, Hanson, & Thornton, 2003), five (COVR; Monahan et al., 2005), and nine (VRAG; Harris, Rice, & Quinsey, 1993) illustrate this range. Each category is associated with a mean, which represents the percentage of individuals within that category who have been detected as violent during the derivation research. It is also associated with a 95% confidence interval, expressing the range within which the true mean is estimated (with 95% confidence) to fall. Ideally such confidence intervals should be narrow, reflecting a strong likelihood that the identified mean represents the performance of that category in a meaningful way. For example, a 95% confidence interval of 48%–52% means that "50%" is better representative than it would be when the confidence interval is wide (e.g., 40%–60%) or extremely wide (e.g., 20%–80%). Narrower confidence intervals are more likely when the sizes of the derivation and validation samples are larger. Well-validated actuarial measures have narrower confidence intervals. If a measure has five risk categories but the confidence intervals surrounding some of the categories overlap, then the evaluator can be less certain about the specific category into which the score should be placed—which affects the conclusions that can be drawn about risk level.

## Special Issues in Testimony

There are a number of considerations that arise regarding expert testimony on risk assessment. To some extent, these also apply in earlier phases of the FMHA risk assessment. They can be summarized as follows:

1. Distinguish risk assessment performed for treatment purposes from that conducted for forensic purposes (see Heilbrun, 2001). In treatment contexts, there are ongoing opportunities to gather additional information, observe responses and changes, and revise the appraisal of risks, needs, and responsivity.

2. Describe all sources of information, and note consistency across sources. When possible, use orthogonal sources of third party information in which the weaknesses of one source are complemented by the strengths of another (Kraemer et al., 2003).

3. Select psychological tests for relevance and reliability. Be prepared to describe in testimony the reliability and validity applicable to each, including the derivation and validation research. Further, be prepared to

describe the limitations on each test, including when it was published, the confidence intervals associated with categories, and the similarity of the derivation and validation samples to the individual being evaluated.

4. Select specialized risk assessment measures for relevance and reliability. Is the outcome associated with the measure comparable to the outcome(s) of interest in the FMHA risk assessment? Be prepared to describe in testimony the reliability and validity applicable to each, including the derivation and validation research. Further, be prepared to describe the limitations on each test, including when it was published, the confidence intervals associated with categories, and the similarity of the derivation and validation samples to the individual being evaluated.

5. Make conclusions and opinions about risk assessment contextually relevant. Carefully consider the questions posed by the law. Legal outcomes (e.g., "dangerousness") are typically much broader than violence or violent offending, and may include any criminal offending (*Jones v. United States*, 1983).

6. Identify the prediction and risk reduction elements of the legal question. If a prediction tool is used, then gather information about dynamic risk factors/criminogenic needs from other sources (e.g., dynamic risk tool, anamnestic interview, collateral information) if a risk reduction opinion is needed.

7. Do not alter the numbers obtained when administering an actuarial tool. If the evaluator's final conclusion regarding risk differs from the category yielded by the actuarial tool, cite the obtained category and describe the reasoning for deviating.

8. All sources are not equal. Consider source credibility. Two specialized risk measures that are highly correlated and with overlapping content do not count as separate, independent measures of risk.

chapter **7**

9. Be prepared to explain the science underlying the development of a given specialized tool. A lay version of the derivation/validation process, and statistical techniques such as logistic regression and tree-based analysis, should be provided upon request.

10. Use risk communication language and concepts that are appropriate to the appraisal and conclusions. Actuarial tools should be conveyed in nomothetic language (frequencies or probabilities), and include information about the group(s) to whom the individual is being compared. Conclusions should incorporate idiographic influences, and be expressed in terms of this particular individual.

## Answering the "Ultimate Legal Question"

Whether the evaluating clinician should answer the ultimate legal question (i.e., offer an ultimate issue opinion) has been debated extensively within the field. The arguments pro (Rogers & Ewing, 1989, 2003) and con (Melton et al., 1987, 1997, 2007; Morse, 1978, 2008; Tillbrook, Mumley, & Grisso, 2003) have been expressed vigorously over the years, and the debate has not yielded a widely accepted intermediate position.

However, the process of FMHA has advanced substantially during the years in which the ultimate issue question has been debated. One of the earliest-noted problems with ultimate issue conclusions was their inscrutability—a report that offered a limited description of data and reasoning made it difficult for the reader to discern why the evaluator had reached the legal conclusion that he did. Such reports were criticized as both brief and conclusory. But the fields of forensic psychology and forensic psychiatry have made it clear that data and reasoning are important (AAPL, 2005; Committee on Ethical Guidelines for Forensic Psychologists, 1991), and there have been numerous advances in other relevant FMHA domains (Heilbrun et al., 2008). Consequently, the ultimate issue debate has been reframed in the context of these advances. Even reports in which the ultimate legal question is answered should no longer be brief and conclusory.

This ultimate issue debate applies in various ways to risk assessment. FMHA risk assessment is conducted to address a variety of legal questions. In some (e.g., Sexually Violent Predator [SVP] evaluations), the question of whether the defendant should be adjudicated as an SVP is driven almost entirely by the risk that he will commit

**BEST PRACTICE**

If answering the ultimate legal question, draw a clear distinction between your opinion as a forensic evaluator and the legal decision to be made by the court.

future sexual offenses. In others (e.g., civil commitment), the risk of future violence to others is one of several considerations, including risk of harm to self and declining voluntary commitment, that must be weighed in determining whether the individual should be involuntarily hospitalized. In yet others (e.g., continuing hospitalization commitment as an insanity acquittee), the risk of violence *and* the response to risk-reducing interventions (particularly in a less structured setting than a hospital) are considered together as part of the legal question of continued involuntary hospitalization.

So one consideration is how closely the violence risk assessment and ultimate legal question resemble one another. It is easier for the legal decision maker to follow the sequence from risk assessment to legal conclusion when the two are similar, as in SVP proceedings. However close the risk appraisal might be to the ultimate legal question, the forensic clinician is still not able to answer the "how much is enough?" question (Tillbrook, Mumley, & Grisso, 2003) without going beyond the bounds of scientific and forensic expertise.

Practical considerations count as well, however. If required by statute or court-ordered to respond, the forensic clinician may have no viable alternative to answering the ultimate legal question. In such cases, the report or testimony may include one of several indications that the distinction between the forensic evaluator and the legal decision maker is recognized by

- offering a sentence prior to the legal opinion that notes this explicitly (e.g., "I recognize and respect that the court will make the legal decision in this matter");

- designating a subsection of the report for the ultimate legal opinion that is separate from the section containing other opinions;
- indicating that it is her "clinical opinion";
- distinguishing the elements of the legal opinion from those of other opinions cited in the report.

For example, the report could include language similar to the following: "Based on my full evaluation, it is my opinion that Mr. X's probability for being rearrested for a sexual offense within 1 year following release is approximately 50%. Whether this risk is sufficient to justify his adjudication as a Sexually Violent Predator is not a scientific or clinical question. However, since I have been asked to answer this legal question, I would add that (in my *clinical* opinion) this risk is sufficient to justify SVP adjudication."

## Conclusion

While risk assessment is conducted in a variety of contexts, this book has focused on evaluations performed in legal settings. FMHA risk assessment is similar in many respects to other kinds of forensic assessments. "Best practice" in this kind of risk assessment incorporates the considerations described in this final chapter, and the preceding six. Ultimately, however, it also requires attention to the influences specific to particular kinds of risk assessment evaluations conducted in legal contexts.

# References

Ægosdóttir, S., White, M. J., Spengler, P, Maugherman, L., Cook, R., Nichols, C., et al. (2006). The meta-analysis of clinical judgment project: Fifty-six years of accumulated research on clinical versus statistical prediction. *The Counseling Psychologist, 34*, 341–382.

American Academy of Psychiatry and the Law. (2005). *Ethics guidelines for the practice of forensic psychiatry.* Bloomfield, CT: Author.

American Bar Association (1989). *Criminal justice mental health standards.* Washington, DC: Author.

American Psychiatric Association. (1982). *Brief amicus curiae, Barefoot v. Estelle.* Retrieved September 15, 2008 from http://archive.psych.org/edu/other_res/lib_archives/archives/amicus/82-6080.pdf

American Psychiatric Association. (2000). *Diagnostic and statistical manual of mental disorders* (4th ed., Text rev.). Washington, DC: Author.

American Psychiatric Association. (2008). *Principles of medical ethics with annotations especially applicable to psychiatry.* Washington, DC: AU.

American Psychological Association (2002). Ethical principles of psychologists and code of conduct. *American Psychologist, 57*, 1060–1073.

Andrews, D., & Bonta, J. (2001). *Level of Service Inventory-Revised (LSI-R): User's manual.* Toronto: Multi-Health Systems.

Andrews, D., & Bonta. J. (2006). *The psychology of criminal conduct* (4th ed.). Newark, NJ: Lexis Nexis/Mathew Bender.

Andrews, D., Bonta, J., & Hoge, R. (1990). Classification for effective rehabilitation: Rediscovering psychology. *Criminal Justice and Behavior, 17*, 19–52.

Andrews, D., Bonta, J., & Wormith, J. (2006). Recent past and near future of risk/need assessment. *Crime and Delinquency, 52*, 7–27.

Andrews, D., & Hoge, R. (in press). *Evaluation for risk of violence in juveniles.* New York: Oxford University Press.

Appelbaum, P., & Gutheil, T. (2007). *Clinical handbook of psychiatry and the law* (4th ed.). Baltimore: Lippincott Williams & Wilkins.

Boer, D., Hart, S., Kropp, R., & Webster, C. (1997). *Manual for the sexual violence risk-20.* Simon Fraser University: The Mental Health, Law, & Policy Institute, Burnaby, BC.

Bonta, J., Law, M., & Hanson, K. (1998). The prediction of criminal and violent recidivism among mentally disordered offenders: A meta-analysis. *Psychological Bulletin, 123*, 123–142.

Borum, R. (1996). Improving the clinical practice of violence risk assessment: Technology, guidelines, and training. *American Psychologist, 51*, 945–956.

Borum, R., Bartels, P., & Forth, A. (2005). *Structured Assessment of Violence Risk in Youth.* Lutz, FL: PAR.

Borum, R. & Grisso, T. (1996). Establishing standards for criminal forensic reports: An empirical analysis. *Bulletin of the American Academy of Psychiatry and Law, 24*, 297–317.

Borum, R., & Reddy, M. (2001). Assessing violence risk in *Tarasoff* situations: A fact-based model of inquiry. *Behavioral Sciences and the Law, 19*, 375–385.

Brennan, T., & Oliver, W. (2000). *Evaluation of reliability and validity of COMPAS scales: National aggregate sample.* Traverse City, MI: Northpointe Institute for Public Management.

Brodsky, S. (1991). *Testifying in court: Guidelines and maxims for the expert witness.* Washington, DC: American Psychological Association.

Brodsky, S. (1999). *The expert expert witness: More maxims and guidelines for testifying in court.* Washington, DC: American Psychological Association.

Brodsky, S. (2004). *Coping with cross-examination and other pathways to effective testimony.* Washington, DC: American Psychological Association.

Catchpole, R., & Gretton, H. (2003). The predictive validity of risk assessment with violent young offenders: A 1-year examination of criminal outcome. *Criminal Justice and Behavior, 30*, 688–708.

Christy, A., Douglas, K., Otto, R., & Petrila, J. (2004). Juveniles evaluated incompetent to proceed: Characteristics and quality of mental health professionals' evaluations. *Professional Psychology: Research and Practice, 35*, 380–388.

Committee on Ethical Guidelines for Forensic Psychologists. (1991). Specialty guidelines for forensic psychologists. *Law and Human Behavior, 15*, 655– 665.

Cooke, D., Wozniak, E., & Johnstone, L. (2008). Casting light on prison violence in Scotland: Evaluating the impact of situational risk factors. *Criminal Justice and Behavior, 35*, 1065–1078.

Cornell, D. (2003). Guidelines for responding to student threats of violence. *Journal of Educational Administration, 41*, 705–719.

Cornell, D. (2006). *School violence: Fears versus facts.* New York: Routledge.

Cunningham, M. (in press). *Evaluation for capital sentencing.* New York: Oxford University Press.

Dahle, K. P. (2006). Strengths and limitations of actuarial prediction of criminal reoffence in a German prison sample: A comparative study of LSI-R, HCR-20 and PCL-R. *International Journal of Law and Psychiatry, 29*, 341–442.

Dawes, R. (1979). The robust beauty of improper linear models. *American Psychologist, 34*, 571–582.

de Vogel, V., & de Ruiter, C. (2005). The HCR-20 in personality disordered female offenders: A comparison with a matched sample of males. *Clinical Psychology and Psychotherapy, 21*, 226–240.

de Vogel, V., & de Ruiter, C. (2006). Structured professional judgment of violence risk in forensic clinical practice: A prospective study into the predictive validity of the Dutch HCR-20. *Psychology, Crime & Law, 12*, 321–336.

de Vogel, V., de Ruiter, C., van Beek, D., & Mead, G. (2004). Predictive validity of the SVR-20 and Static-99 in a Dutch sample of treated sex offenders. *Law and Human Behavior, 28*, 235–251.

Douglas, K., & Kropp, P. R. (2002). A prevention-based paradigm for violence risk assessment: Clinical and research applications. *Criminal Justice and Behavior, 29*, 617–658.

Douglas, K., Ogloff, J., Nicholls, T., & Grant, I. (1999). Assessing risk for violence among psychiatric patients: The HCR-20 violence risk assessment scheme and the Psychopathy Checklist: Screening Version. *Journal of Consulting and Clinical Psychology, 67*, 917–930.

Douglas, K., & Skeem, J. (2005). Violence risk assessment: Getting specific about being dynamic. *Psychology, Public Policy, and Law, 11*, 347–383.

Douglas, K., & Webster, C. (1999). The HCR-20 violence risk assessment scheme: Concurrent validity in a sample of incarcerated offenders. *Criminal Justice and Behavior, 26*, 3–19.

Douglas, K., Webster, C., Hart, S., Eaves, D., & Ogloff, J. (2001). *HCR-20 violence risk management companion guide.* Burnaby, BC: Mental Health, Law, and Policy Institute, Simon Fraser University.

Douglas, K., Yeomans, M., & Boer, D. (2005). Comparative validity analysis of multiple measures of violence risk in a general population sample of criminal offenders. *Criminal Justice and Behavior, 32*, 479–510.

Dvoskin, J., & Heilbrun, K. (2001). Risk assessment and release decision-making: Toward resolving the great debate. *Journal of the American Academy of Psychiatry and the Law, 29*, 6–10.

Enebrink, P., Langstrom, N., & Gumpert, C. (2006). Predicting aggressive and disruptive behavior in referred 6 to 12-year-old boys: Prospective validation of the EARL-20B Risk/Needs Checklist. *Assessment, 13*, 356–367.

Epperson, D., Kaul, J., Huot, S., Goldman, R., & Alexander, W. (2003). *Minnesota Sex Offender Screening Tool-Revised (MnSOST-R) technical paper: Development, validation, and recommended risk level cut scores.* Currently unpublished manuscript retrieved 9-4-08 from <http://www.psychology.iastate.edu/~dle/TechUpdatePaper12-03.pdf>

Ewing, C. (1983). "Dr. Death" and the case for an ethical ban on psychiatric and psychological predictions of dangerousness in capital sentencing proceedings. *American Journal of Law and Medicine, 8*, 407–428.

Ewing, C. (1991). Preventive detention and execution: The constitutionality of punishing future crimes. *Law and Human Behavior, 15*, 139–163.

Fass, T., Heilbrun, K., DeMatteo, D., & Fretz, R. (2008). The LSI-R and the COMPAS: Validation data on two risk-needs tools. *Criminal Justice and Behavior, 35*, 1095–1108.

Felthous, A., & Gunn, J. (1999). Forensic psychiatric reports. *Current Opinion in Psychiatry, 12*, 643–645.

Forth, A., Kosson, D., & Hare, R. (2003). *Psychopathy Checklist: Version.* Ontario, Canada: Multi-Health Systems.

Gendreau, P., Goggin, C., & Smith, P. (2002). Is the PCL-R really the "unparalleled" measure of offender risk? A lesson in knowledge cumulation. *Criminal Justice and Behavior, 29*, 397–426.

Gore, K. (2008). Adjusted actuarial assessment of sex offenders: The impact of clinical overrides on predictive accuracy. *Dissertation Abstracts International: Section B: The Sciences and Engineering, 68*(7-B), 4824.

Grann, M., & Langstrom, N. (2007). Actuarial assessment of violence risk: To weigh or not to weigh. *Criminal Justice and Behavior, 34*, 22–36.

Greene, E., Heilbrun, K., Fortune, W., & Nietzel, M. (2006). *Wrightsman's psychology and the legal system* (6th ed.). Belmont, CA: Wadsworth.

Grisso, T. (1986). *Evaluating competencies.* New York: Plenum.

Grisso, T. (2003). *Evaluating competencies* (2nd ed.). New York: Kluwer Academic/Plenum.

Grisso, T., & Appelbaum, P. (1992). Is it unethical to offer predictions of future violent behavior? *Law and Human Behavior, 16*, 621–633.

Grove, W., & Meehl, P. (1996). Comparative efficiency of informal (subjective, impressionistic) and formal (mechanical, algorithmic) prediction procedures: The clinical-statistical controversy. *Psychology, Public Policy, and Law, 2*, 293–323.

Grove, W., Zald, D., Lebow, B., Snitz, B., & Nelson, C. (2000). Clinical versus mechanical prediction: A meta-analysis. *Psychological Assessment, 12*, 19–30.

Hanson, R., & Thornton, D. (1999). *Static 99: Improving actuarial risk assessments for sex offenders.* Ottawa: Ministry of the Solicitor General of Canada.

Harris, A., Phenix, A., Hanson, R. K., & Thornton, D. (2003). STATIC-99 coding rules: Revised-2003. Retrieved July 21, 2008 from http://ww2.ps-sp.gc.ca/publications/corrections/pdf/Static-99-coding-Rules_e.pdf

Harris, G., & Rice, M. (2007). Characterizing the value of actuarial violence risk assessments. *Criminal Justice and Behavior, 34*, 1638–1658.

Harris, G., Rice, M., & Cormier, C. (2002). Prospective replication of the Violence Risk Appraisal Guide in predicting violent recidivism among forensic patients. *Law and Human Behavior, 26*, 377–394.

Harris, G., Rice, M., Quinsey, V., Lalumiere, M., Boer, D., & Lang, C. (2003). A multi-site comparison of actuarial risk instruments for sex offenders. *Psychological Assessment: A Journal of Consulting and Clinical Psychology, 15*, 413–425.

Hart, S., Michie, C., & Cooke, D. (2007). The precision of actuarial risk assessment instruments: Evaluating the "margins of error" of group versus individual predictions of violence. *British Journal of Psychiatry, 190*, s60–s65.

Hecker, T., & Steinberg, L. (2002). Psychological evaluation at juvenile court disposition. *Professional Psychology: Research and Practice, 33*, 300–306.

Heilbrun, K. (1997). Prediction vs. management models relevant to risk assessment: The importance of legal context. *Law and Human Behavior, 21*, 347–359.

Heilbrun, K. (2001). *Principles of forensic mental health assessment.* New York: Kluwer Academic/Plenum.

Heilbrun, K., & Collins, S. (1995). Evaluations of trial competency and mental state at the time of the offense: Report characteristics. *Professional Psychology: Research and Practice, 26*, 61–67.

Heilbrun, K., Douglas, K., & Yasuhara, K. (in press). Violence risk assessment: Core controversies. In J. Skeem, K. Douglas, & S. Lilienfeld (Eds.), *Psychological science in the courtroom: Controversies and consensus.* New York: Guilford.

Heilbrun, K., Dvoskin, J., Hart, S., & McNiel, D. (1999). Violence risk communication: Implications for research, policy, and practice. *Health, Risk, and Society, 1*, 91–106.

Heilbrun, K., Goldstein, N., & Redding, R. (Eds.) (2005). *Juvenile delinquency: Prevention, assessment, and intervention.* New York: Oxford University Press.

Heilbrun, K., Grisso, T., & Goldstein, A. (2008). *Foundations of forensic mental health assessment.* New York: Oxford University Press.Heilbrun, K., Marczyk, G., & DeMatteo, D. (2002). *Forensic mental health assessment: A casebook.* New York: Oxford University Press.

Heilbrun, K., Rogers, R., & Otto, R. (2002). Forensic assessment: Current status and future directions. In J. Ogloff (Ed.), *Psychology and law: Reviewing the discipline* (pp. 120–147). New York: Kluwer Academic/Plenum.

Heilbrun, K., Warren, J., & Picarello, K. (2003). Use of third party information in forensic assessment. In A. Goldstein (Ed.), *Comprehensive handbook of psychology: Vol. 11. Forensic psychology* (pp. 69–86). New York: Wiley.

Heilbrun, K., Yasuhara, K., & Shah, S. (in press). Violence risk assessment tools: Overview and critical analysis. In R. Otto & K. Douglas (Eds.), *Handbook of violence risk assessment tools.* New York: Routledge.

Hoge, R., & Andrews, D. (2002). *The Youth Level of Service/Case Management Inventory manual and scoring key.* Toronto, Ontario, Canada: Multi-Health Systems.

Kraemer, H., Kazdin, A., Offord, D., Kessler, R., Jensen, P., & Kupfer, D. (1997). Coming to terms with the terms of risk. *Archives of General Psychiatry, 54*, 337–343.

Kraemer, H., Measelle, J., Ablow, J., Essex, M., Boyce, W., & Kupfer, D. (2003). A new approach to multiple informants: Mixing and matching context and perspectives. *American Journal of Psychiatry, 160*, 1566–1577.

Kroner, D., Mills, J., & Reddon, J. (2005). A coffee can, factor analysis, and prediction of antisocial behavior: The structure of criminal risk. *International Journal of Law and Psychiatry, 28*, 360–374.

Kropp, P. R., & Hart, S. (2000). The Spousal Assault Risk Assessment (SARA) guide: Reliability and validity in adult male offenders. *Law and Human Behavior, 24*, 101–118.

Lander, T., & Heilbrun, K. (in press). The content and quality of forensic mental health assessment: Validation of a principles-based approach. *International Journal of Forensic Mental Health Services.*

Leistico, A., Salekin, R., DeCosta, J., & Rogers, R. (2008). A large-scale meta-analysis relating the Hare measures of psychopathy to antisocial conduct. *Law and Human Behavior, 32*, 28–45.

Loftus, E. (1992). When a lie becomes memory's truth: Memory distortion after exposure to misinformation. *Psychological Science, 1*, 121–123.

Loftus, E. (1997). Creating false memories. *Scientific American, 277*, 70–75.

McGowan, M. (2007). The predictive validity of violence risk assessment within educational settings. *Dissertation Abstracts International: Section A: Humanities and Social Sciences, 68*(3-A), 876. McGrath, R. (2008). Predictor combination in binary decision-making situations. *Psychological Assessment, 20*, 195–205.

McNiel, D., & Binder, R. (1994). Screening for risk of inpatient violence: Validation of an actuarial tool. *Law and Human Behavior, 18*, 579–586.

Meehl, P. E. (1957). When shall we use our heads instead of the formula? *Journal of Counseling Psychology, 4*, 268–273.

Megargee, E. (1982). Psychological determinants and correlates of criminal violence. In M. Wolfgang and N. Weiner (Eds.), *Criminal violence* (pp. 81–170). Beverly Hills, CA: Sage.

Meloy, J. R. (Ed.) (1998). *The psychology of stalking: Clinical and forensic perspectives.* San Diego, CA: Academic Press.

Meloy, J. R. (2000). *Violence risk and threat assessment: A practical guide for mental health and criminal justice professionals.* San Diego, CA: Specialized Training Services.

Melton, G., Petrila, J., Poythress, N., & Slobogin, C. (1987). *Psychological evaluations for the courts: A handbook for mental health professionals and lawyers.* New York: Guilford.

Melton, G., Petrila, J., Poythress, N., & Slobogin, C. (1997). *Psychological evaluations for the courts: A handbook for mental health professionals and lawyers* (2nd ed.). New York: Guilford.

Melton, G., Petrila, J., Poythress, N., & Slobogin, C. (2007). *Psychological evaluations for the courts: A handbook for mental health professionals and lawyers* (3rd ed.). New York: Guilford.

Meyers, J., & Schmidt, F. (2008). Predictive validity of the Structured Assessment for Violence Risk in Youth (SAVRY) with juvenile offenders. *Criminal Justice and Behavior, 35*, 344–355.

Monahan, J. (1981). *Predicting violent behavior: An assessment of clinical techniques.* Beverly Hills, CA: Sage.

Monahan, J. (1984). The prediction of violent behavior: Toward a second generation of theory and policy. *American Journal of Psychiatry, 141*, 10–15.

Monahan, J. (1993). Limiting therapist exposure to *Tarasoff* liability: Guidelines for risk containment. *American Psychologist, 48*, 242–250.

Monahan, J. (2008). Structured risk assessment of violence. In R. Simon and K. Tardiff (Eds.), *Textbook of violence assessment and management* (pp. 17–33). Washington, DC: American Psychiatric Publishing.

Monahan, J., & Silver, E. (2003). Judicial decision thresholds for violence risk management. *International Journal of Forensic Mental Health, 2*, 1–6.

Monahan, J., & Steadman, H. (1994) (Eds.). *Violence and mental disorder: Developments in risk assessment.* Chicago: University of Chicago Press.

Monahan, J., & Steadman, H. J. (1996). Violent storms and violent people: How meteorology can inform risk communication in mental health law. *American Psychologist, 51*, 931–938.

Monahan, J., Steadman, H., Robbins, P. C., Appelbaum, P., Banks, S., Grisso, T., et al. (2005). Prospective validation of the multiple iterative classification tree model of violence risk assessment. *Psychiatric Services, 56*, 810–815.

Monahan, J., Steadman, H., Silver, E., Appelbaum, P., Robbins, P. C., Mulvey, E., et al. (2001). *Rethinking risk assessment: The MacArthur study of mental disorder and violence.* New York: Oxford University Press.

Morse, S. (1978). Law and mental health professionals: The limits of expertise. *Professional Psychology, 9*, 389–399.

Morse, S. (2008). The ethics of forensic practice: Reclaiming the wasteland. *Journal of the American Academy of Psychiatry and the Law, 36*, 206–217.

Mossman, D. (1994). Assessing predictions of violence: Being accurate about accuracy. *Journal of Consulting and Clinical Psychology, 62*, 783–792.

Mossman, D. (2007). Avoiding errors about "margins of error." *British Journal of Psychiatry, 191*, 561.

National Research Council. (1989). *Improving risk communication.* Washington, DC: The National Academies Press.

Nicholson, R., & Norwood, S. (2000). The quality of forensic psychological assessments, reports, and testimony: Acknowledging the gap between promise and practice. *Law and Human Behavior, 24*, 9–44.

Ogloff, J., & Daffern, M. (2006). The dynamic appraisal of situational aggression: An instrument to assess risk for imminent aggression in psychiatric inpatients. *Behavioral Sciences and the Law, 24*, 799–813.

Otto, R. (1992). The prediction of dangerous behavior: A review and analysis of "second generation" research. *Forensic Reports, 5*, 103–134.

Otto, R., & Borum, R. (1997). *Assessing and managing violence risk: A workshop for clinicians.* Tampa, FL: Louis de la Parte Florida Mental Health Institute, University of South Florida.

Otto, R., & Douglas, K. (Eds.) (in press). *Handbook of violence risk assessment tools*. New York: Routledge.

Petrella, R., & Poythress, N. (1983). The quality of forensic evaluations: An interdisciplinary study. *Journal of Consulting and Clinical Psychology, 51*, 76–85.

Pinals, D., & Mossman, D. (in preparation). *Evaluation for civil commitment*. New York: Oxford University Press.

Quinsey, V., Harris, G., Rice, M., & Cormier, C. (1998). *Violent offenders: Appraising and managing risk*. Washington, DC: American Psychological Association.

Quinsey, V., Harris, G., Rice, M., & Cormier, C. (2006). *Violent offenders: Appraising and managing risk* (2nd ed.). Washington, DC: American Psychological Association.

Rice, M., & Harris, G. (1995). Violent recidivism: Assessing predictive validity. *Journal of Consulting and Clinical Psychology, 63*, 737–748.

Rice, M., Harris, G., & Cormier, C. (1992). Evaluation of a maximum security therapeutic community for psychopaths and other mentally disordered offenders. *Law and Human Behavior, 16*, 399–412.

Rice, M., Harris, G., Lang, C., & Bell, V. (1990). Recidivism among male insanity acquittees. *Journal of Psychiatry and Law, 18*, 379–403.

Richter, D., & Whittington, R. (Eds.) (2006). *Violence in mental health settings*. New York: Springer.

Rogers, R. (1992). *Structured Interview of Reported Symptoms*. Odessa, FL: Psychological Assessment Resources.

Rogers, R., & Ewing, C. (1989). Ultimate opinion proscriptions: A cosmetic fix and a plea for empiricism. *Law and Human Behavior, 13*, 357–374.

Rogers, R., & Ewing, C. (2003). The prohibition of ultimate opinions: A misguided enterprise. *Journal of Forensic Psychology Practice, 3*, 65–76.

Silver, E. (2001). *Mental illness and violence: The importance of neighborhood context*. El Paso, TX: LFB Scholarly Publishing.

Silver, E., Mulvey, E., & Monahan, J. (1999). Assessing violence risk among discharged psychiatric patients: Toward an ecological approach. *Law and Human Behavior, 23*, 237–255.

Simon, R., & Gold, L. (Eds.) (2004a). *Textbook of forensic psychiatry*. Washington, DC: American Psychiatric Publishing.

Simon, R., & Gold, L. (2004b). Psychiatric diagnosis in litigation. In R. Simon & L. Gold (Eds.), *Textbook of forensic psychiatry* (pp. 117–138). Washington, DC: American Psychiatric Publishing.

Sjöstedt, G., & Långström, N. (2002). Assessment of risk for criminal recidivism among rapists: A comparison of four different measures. *Psychology, Crime and Law, 8*, 25–40.

Skeem, J., Schubert, C., Odgers, C., Mulvey, E., Gardner, W., & Lidz, C. (2006). Psychiatric symptoms and community violence among high-risk patients: A test of the relationship at the weekly level. *Journal of Consulting and Clinical Psychology, 74*, 967–979.

Slovic, P., & Monahan, J. (1995). Probability, danger and coercion: A study of risk perception and decision making in mental health law. *Law and Human Behavior, 19,* 49–65.

Slovic, P., Monahan, J., & MacGregor, D. (2000). Violence risk assessment and risk communication: The effects of using actual cases, providing instruction, and employing probability versus frequency formats. *Law and Human Behavior, 24,* 271–296.

Steadman, H. (1982). A situational approach to violence. *International Journal of Law and Psychiatry, 5,* 171–186.

Steadman, H., Monahan, J., Appelbaum, P., Grisso, T., Mulvey, E., Roth, L., et al. (1994). Designing a new generation of risk assessment research. In J. Monahan and H. Steadman (Eds.), *Violence and mental disorder: Developments in risk assessment* (pp. 297–318). Chicago: University of Chicago Press.

Steadman, H., Mulvey, E., Monahan, J., Robbins, P., Appelbaum, P., Grisso, T., et al. (1998). Violence by people discharged from acute psychiatric inpatient facilities and by others in the same neighborhoods. *Archives of General Psychiatry, 55,* 1–9.

Tillbrook, C., Mumley, D., & Grisso, T. (2003). Avoiding expert opinions on the ultimate legal question: The case for integrity. *Journal of Forensic Psychology Practice, 3,* 77–87.

Tolman, A., & Mullendore, K. (2003). Risk evaluations for the courts: Is service quality a function of specialization? *Professional Psychology: Research and Practice, 34,* 225–232.

Viljoen, J.L., Scalora, M., Cuadra, L., Bader, S., Chávez, V., Ullman, D., & Lawrence, L. (2008). Assessing risk for violence in adolescents who have sexually offended: A comparison of the J-SOAP-II, J-SORRAT-II, and SAVRY. *Criminal Justice and Behavior, 35,* 5–23.

Walters, G. (2003). Predicting criminal justice outcomes with the Psychopathy Checklist and Lifestyle Criminality Screening Form: A meta-analytic comparison. *Behavioral Sciences & the Law, 21,* 89–102.

Wells, G., & Olson, E. (2003). Eyewitness testimony. *Annual Review of Psychology, 54,* 277–295.

Welsh, J. Schmidt, F., McKinnon, L., Chattha, H., & Meyers, J. (2008). A comparative study of adolescent risk assessment instruments: Predictive and incremental validity. *Assessment, 15,* 104–115.Wilson, E. (1927). Probable inference, the law of succession, and statistical inference. *Journal of the American Statistical Association, 22,* 209–212.

Witt, P., & Conroy, M.A. (2008). *Evaluation of sexually violent predators.* New York: Oxford University Press.

# Tests and Specialized Tools

COVR: Classification of Violence Risk (Monahan, Steadman, Appelbaum et al., 2005)

HCR-20: Historical, Clinical, Risk Management-20 (Webster, Douglas, Eaves, & Hart, 1997)

LCSF: Lifestyle Criminality Screening Form (Walters, White, & Denney, 1991)

LSI-R: Level of Service Inventory-Revised (Andrews & Bonta, 1995)

LS/CMI: Level of Service/Case Management Inventory (Andrews, Bonta, & Wormith, 2004)

MCMI-III: Millon Clinical Multiaxial Inventory-III (Millon, Davis, & Millon, 1997)

MMPI-2: Minnesota Multiphasic Personality Inventory-2 (Tellegan, Ben-Porath, McNulty, Arbisi, Graham, & Kaemmer, 2003)

NAS-PI: Novaco Anger Scale and Provocation Inventory (Novaco, 2003)

PAI: Personality Assessment Inventory (Morey, 2007)

PCL-R: Psychopathy Checklist-Revised (Hare, 1991, 2003)

PCL-SV: Psychopathy Checklist-Screening Version (Hart, Cox, & Hare, 1995)

VRAG: Violence Risk Appraisal Guide (Harris, Rice, & Quinsey, 1993)

# References for Tests and Specialized Tools

Andrews, D., & Bonta, J. (1995). *The level of service inventory-revised: user's manual*. North Tonawanda, NY: Multi-Health Systems.

Andrews, D., Bonta, J., & Wormith, J. (2004). *The level of service/case management inventory user's manual*. North Tonawanda, NY: Multi-Health Systems.

Hare, R. (1991). *The Hare Psychopathy Checklist-Revised*. Toronto, ON: Multi-Health Systems.

Harris, G., Rice, M., & Quinsey, V. (1993). Violent recidivism of mentally disordered offenders: The development of a statistical prediction instrument. *Criminal Justice and Behavior, 20*, 315–335.

Hart, S., Cox, D., & Hare, R. (1995). *The Hare Psychopathy Checklist: Screening Version (PCL:SV)*. North Tonawanda, NY: Multi-Health Systems.

Millon, T., Davis, R., & Millon, C. (1997). *Millon Clinical Multiaxial Inventory-III manual* (2nd ed.). Minneapolis, MN: National Computer Systems.

Monahan, J., Steadman, H., Appelbaum, P., Grisso, T., Mulvey, E., Roth, L., et al. (2005). *Classification of violence risk: Professional manual*. Lutz, FL: Psychological Assessment Resources.

Morey, L. C. (2007). *Personality Assessment Inventory professional manual* (2nd ed.). Lutz, FL: Psychological Assessment Resources.

Novaco, R. (2003). *Novaco Anger Scale and Provocation Inventory (NAS-PI).* Los Angeles: Western Psychological Services.

Tellegan, A., Ben-Porath, Y., McNulty, J., Arbisi, P., Graham, J., & Kaemmer, B. (2003). *The MMPI-2 restructured clinical scales: Development, validation, and interpretation.* Minneapolis, MN: University of Minnesota Press.

Walters, G. D., White, T. W., & Denney, D. (1991). The lifestyle criminality screening form: preliminary data. *Criminal Justice and Behavior, 18,* 406–418.

Webster, C., Douglas, K., Eaves, D., & Hart, S. (1997). *HCR-20: Assessing risk for violence* (Version 2). Burnaby, BC: Mental Health, Law, and Policy Institute, Simon Fraser University.

# Cases and Statutes

Abdul-Kabir *v.* Quarterman, 127 S. Ct. 1654 (2007).

Barefoot *v.* Estelle, 463 U.S. 880 (1983).

Estelle *v.* Smith, 451 U.S. 454 (1981).

Foucha *v.* Louisiana, 504 U.S. 71 (1992).

Gregg *v.* Georgia, 428 U.S. 153 (1976).

Jones *v.* United States, 463 U.S. 354 (1983).

Jurek *v.* Texas, 428 U.S. 263 (1976).

Kansas *v.* Hendricks, 521 U.S. 346 (1997).

Lessard *v.* Schmidt, 349 F. Supp. 1078 (1973).

O'Connor *v.* Donaldson, 422 U.S. 563 (1975).

Profitt *v.* Florida, 428 U.S. 242 (1976).

Satterwhite *v.* Texas, 486 U.S. 249 (1988).

Tarasoff *v.* Regents of University of California, 17 Cal.3d 425 (1974).

Tarasoff *v.* Regents of University of California, 551 P.2d 334 (1976).

Vitek *v.* Jones, 445 U.S. 480 (1980).

# Key Terms

**actuarial risk assessment:** approach to risk assessment in which information is obtained on a number of specified predictor variables and then combined using a preestablished "formula" to yield a final risk estimate.

**adjusted actuarial:** adjusting the results of an actuarial prediction through clinical judgment (which is not recommended), as contrasted with adjusting the interpretation of actuarial results (acceptable occasionally but likely to lower overall accuracy if done more than infrequently).

**anamnestic:** approach to risk assessment in which detailed information is obtained from the individual concerning previous target behavior, with the goal of identifying individualized risk factors for the future occurrence of this target behavior.

**clinical contexts:** circumstances in which the individual being assessed is involved in treatment rather than litigation, so risk assessment will be used for treatment planning purposes.

**clinical measures:** psychological tests or instruments that describe characteristics or conditions that are useful in diagnosis and treatment planning but typically would not be considered in a forensic evaluation.

**dangerousness:** a state in which an individual is at increased *risk* to commit *a particular outcome behavior* (aggression or other antisocial behavior) as evidenced by the presence of *risk factors*; often used in legal contexts but less useful for clarity than the term *risk assessment*.

**dynamic risk factors:** variables subject to change over time or through planned intervention that affect an individual's likelihood of some target behavior, such as violence or sexual violence.

**face validity:** the appearance of validity; in social science, one of the weakest forms of validity; in legal contexts, an important form of validity considering the credibility associated with face validity.

**false negative:** a prediction that a specified outcome will not occur when it does, in fact, occur.

**false positive:** a prediction that a specified outcome will occur when it does not, in fact, occur.

**forensic assessment instruments:** specialized tools designed for assessment of the functional legal abilities of direct relevance to legal questions.

**forensically relevant instruments:** psychological tests or instruments that assist in evaluating characteristics or conditions that, although not the focus of legal inquiry, might be considered in a forensic evaluation (e.g., intelligence tests, tests of malingering).

**functional legal capacities:** what an individual must be able to think, say, and do in order to satisfy the specific demands of a particular legal decision.

**habit strength:** the individual's history of a specified target behavior.

**harm:** the consequences of the aggression being predicted.

**idiographic:** data obtained through the investigation of one individual, usually the individual under consideration.

**Incompetent to Stand Trial (IST):** a legal finding in which a given defendant is identified as lacking in the abilities necessary to meaningfully participate in a relevant stage(s) of the proceedings.

**inhibition:** sum of the internal influences (thoughts, feelings, motivations, and the like) that make it less likely that an individual will display violent behavior.

**instigation:** the sum of internal influences that incline an individual toward behaving violently.

**legal contexts:** circumstances in which the individual being assessed is involved in litigation, so risk assessment will be used to inform legal decision-making.

**Needs:** the second of three principles in the RNR model; deficits related to the probability of reoffending outcomes (called *criminogenic* needs in the RNR model).

**nomothetic:** data obtained through the scientific investigation of groups and group differences.

**Not Guilty by Reason of Insanity (NGRI):** a legal determination that an individual will not be held responsible for an act based upon the individual's mental state at the time of the commission of the act; the specific criteria for such a determination are defined by applicable statutes or case law.

**post-sentence *Hendricks* commitments:** civil commitment of sex offenders classified as sexually violent predators (SVPs) following completion of their prison sentences.

**prediction-oriented tools:** risk assessment tools that have been developed solely for the purpose of estimating the risk of future violence committed by the individual being assessed.

**Responsivity:** one of three principles in the RNR model; the individual's likelihood of responding to intervention(s) designed to reduce the risk of criminal reoffending and the related influences that affect such likelihood.

**Risk:** one of three principles in the RNR model; the principle that those most likely to engage in future crime should receive the most intensive intervention and management services.

**risk assessment:** the assessment of risk factors associated with risk level for behavior resulting in harm to others.

**risk factors:** variables empirically associated with the probability that aggression will occur.

**risk level:** the probability that harm will occur.

**risk-needs tools:** risk assessment tools developed both for estimating risk of future target behavior and describing risk-relevant needs which, if addressed, should lower such risk.

**school contexts:** circumstances in which the individual is assessed for risk of harm to others in school, so risk assessment will be used to inform a school decision.

**situation:** factors relevant in risk assessment that are not internal, including location, the presence of others, and the ingestion of drugs or alcohol.

**static risk factors:** variables that are historical or do not change through planned intervention and that are related to an individual's likelihood of some specified target behavior such as violence or sexual violence.

**structured professional judgment:** approach to risk assessment in which the evaluator considers information in a number of specific domains relevant to risk, but then makes a final professional judgment concerning risk without calculating a score or using a specified heuristic.

**threats to protectees:** circumstances in which the individual is assessed for harm to an individual under the specific protection of an agency (e.g., the U.S. President and the Secret Service) or the risk of harm to another individual in a domestic violence context (e.g., a family member as gauged by the police).

**true negative:** a prediction that a specified outcome will not occur when it does not, in fact, occur.

**true positive:** a prediction that a specified outcome will occur when it does, in fact, occur.

**ultimate issue testimony:** testimony in which the expert gives a direct answer to the "ultimate legal question" before the court.

**workplace contexts:** circumstances in which the individual is assessed for risk of harm to others in the workplace, so risk assessment will be used to inform a work decision.

# Index

Note: Locators referring to tables and figures are given with *t* and *f* respectively.

# About the Author

**Kirk Heilbrun**, PhD, is currently Professor and Head of the Department of Psychology, Drexel University. His current research focuses on juvenile and adult offenders, legal decision making, and forensic evaluation associated with such decision-making. He is the author of a number of articles on forensic assessment, violence risk assessment and risk communication, and the treatment of mentally disordered offenders, and has published five books (*Principles of Forensic Mental Health Assessment*, 2001; *Forensic Mental Health Assessment: A Casebook*, with Geff Marczyk and Dave DeMatteo, 2002; *Juvenile Delinquency: Prevention, Assessment, and Intervention*, with Naomi Goldstein and Rich Redding, 2005; *Wrightsman's Psychology and the Legal System*, 6th edition, with Edie Greene, Mike Nietzel, and Bill Fortune, 2006, and *Foundations of Forensic Mental Health Assessment*, with Tom Grisso and Alan Goldstein, 2008). His practice interests also center around forensic assessment, and he directs a clinic within the department in this area. He is board certified in Clinical Psychology and in Forensic Psychology by the American Board of Professional Psychology, and has previously served as president of both the American Psychology—Law Psychology/APA Division 41, and the American Board of Forensic Psychology. He received the 2004 Distinguished Contributions to Forensic Psychology award and the 2009 Beth Clark Award for Distinguished Service from the American Academy of Forensic Psychology.